NAKED
NEW YORK

PARAGON ASSOCIATES, INC.
NEW YORK

NAKED
NEW YORK

———————————by BOB HARRISON

PRINTED IN THE UNITED STATES OF AMERICA
AT THE COLONIAL PRESS INC.

To:

The three women in my life

HELEN · EDITH · JUNE

NAKED
NEW YORK

CONTENTS

▶ ▶ ▶

NAKED
NEW YORK

NAKED
NEW YORK

---

introducing:

NAKED NEW YORK

SHE'S BIG AND bawdy and beautiful. She's night and day, hot and cold, black and white and every shade of gray. She's the millionaire's mistress, the salesman's sweetie, the madam and the whore. She's wild and wicked and wasted, mad and maddening and mysterious, a mixture of hell and heaven in equal parts. She's the itching palm behind the come-on smile, the fine print in the social contract, the pungent punchline to the dirty joke.

She's got stars in her eyes and hay in her hair, but these things can't mask the cashbox she's got for a heart. She's every kiddie's doll—she laughs, she sings, she cries real tears. She's a lady and a tramp at once, and you can buy her and sell her a million times over and never know her at all.

Her name is New York.

Other reporters more capable than ourselves have tackled her. They've attacked her street-by-street, block-by-blazing-block, filling book after book with the shocking truth about every aspect of the biggest big town in the world from the Battery to the Bronx.

They've written chapters galore about Harlem, where mugging is a social sport and heroin addiction is a species of conformity. They've peeked perilously at Greenwich Village, where boys will be girls and girls will be boys and nobody knows the difference. They've covered reams of paper with the inside story of Little Puerto Rico, that Spanish-speaking ghetto that grows and grows, where the streetwalkers do the mambo, where everything's for sale and the price is always right.

And they've worn out typewriters telling the story of the Broadway hustlers, where the fast buck is the only buck there is, where everybody lives high and nobody works for a living. Where everyone will take you as you are . . . or for everything you've got.

That's an old story by now.

But the cheats and the chiselers and the chippies never give up. No sooner do you catch up with one racket than they dream up another. As quick as you handcuff one illegal operation, they've got both hands free . . . and reaching for your wallet. The laws and the reporters are on a merry-go-round that never stops, and the hipsters and tipsters and gypsters have their hot little hands wound around the brass ring.

This is the *new* story.

This is the up-to-the-minute report on how the hustlers hustle in the never-ending search for money and madness, loot and love, dough and dolls. It's as new as tomorrow, as urgent as a drowning man's cry for help. It tells about the new gimmicks and gambits designed to show how easily a fool and his money are parted for keeps. It opens up the methods by which the cheater and the chump get together, making the cheater rich and sending the chump to the poorhouse.

Here are the swindlers and the swells, the babes who scheme and the pimps who outsmart them—all conning their way in the greatest shell game on earth—because larceny is their business.

This is no Cook's tour around Manhattan. This is New York stripped and in the raw!

It's a story that forgets the old stuff, a story that shows you every new wrinkle on the face of the lady named New York. It's a story with no holds barred, that pulls out the stops but never pulls the punches. It's a story that smartens the sophisticate and puts the hayseed hip. It's the last word on a most amazing lady—

It's *Naked New York!*

Scandal in the sky . . .

FLOATING CRAP GAMES IN THE AIR

Broadway's sharpies have come up with a new one, gambling planes which give you four hours of fast play at 9,000 feet . . . And it may well turn out to be as legal as bingo at a church bazaar!

THE BROADWAY GAMBLER is a breed you'll find nowhere else in the world. He lives high, wide and handsome but he toils not. That's strictly for the peasants. As far as he's concerned 9 to 5 means odds, not working hours.

Now he has a new gimmick, a fresh twist on the galloping

15

dominoes. It's the hottest gambit since prohibition went down the constitutional drain—a floating crap game in the air, where the law can't make a pinch and the hoods can't make a heist.

Weather permitting, you can see them any Wednesday or Saturday night at one of the big airports serving metropolitan New York. The men and women rushing to board the big airliner look like any of a hundred other passengers setting off on a trip.

But their destination would have the Wright brothers spinning in their graves. They're heading up into the wild, blue yonder for a date with the dancing dice—where the sky is the limit.

Don't be surprised if you haven't heard of these casinos in the air. They're fresher than the ink on your morning newspaper and still so novel that some of the best legal brains in the country aren't sure, at this point, whether any enforceable law is being broken. Any day now, the dignified Civil Aeronautics Board may be asked to check up on these shenanigans and there's an excellent possibility that it may declare it has no power to so much as shake a finger at the cloudland dice games.

The whole operation is as smooth as the flights guaranteed by the chartered luxury planes which are used in these celestial capers. And it's far more exclusive. For instance, there's no way in the world of applying for a membership in this club. A lover of the rattling ivories has to wait patiently for someone who's already on the inside to nominate him for the honors.

If your qualifications prove okay—and even Dun and Bradstreet couldn't check you more closely—things happen fast. First, you get a card like the one shown on the next page, delivered by the mailman in a plain, white envelope.

No letter of explanation accompanies the above card. That comes later in a telephone call, during which you're given the name of the intimate friend who has recommended you for an evening's entertainment with the galloping dominoes.

It's at this point that those strange little dots on your card—those around the word "Club"—begin to make sense. They're the symbol for the evening's sport—craps, *à la stratosphere*.

Unlike most travelers, you're told not to pack a bag, just bring money. You're given exact instructions as to the airport, date number and departure time, as well as the hour that the specially chartered gambling plane will return.

True to the age-old tradition of floating crap games, the scene of action is never the same. In New York one departure may be from La Guardia field, the next from Idlewild International Airport and a third from New Jersey's Newark or Teterboro fields. Just to make doubly sure of secrecy, the plane never returns directly to the airport from which it took off. If the departure was from Idlewild, for instance, the return will be at Newark or La Guardia.

But that's no inconvenience to members of the ultra-snooty

"Sky-High" Club, since private limousines deliver them to the gate and pick them up when the game's over.

The boys who dreamed up this program thought of everything. Their high-flying casino is a typical 25- or 30-passenger plane as it stands at the loading ramp or taxis into position for the take-off. The interesting changes begin as soon as it has gained altitude and soared out over the Atlantic.

Two stewards appear at the front of the ship, and as the passengers step aside one by one, the seats on one side of the plane are expertly unbolted and hustled to the rear. Then two large suitcases are hauled out and opened to reveal a compact, fold-away craps table which is spread neatly across the tops of the seats remaining on the plane's other side. A stickman takes up his position in the middle of the layout and the next move for the gilt-edge customers is obvious—unfasten your money belts.

Remnants of the old Joe Adonis mob hatched this slick plot for dates in the sky with Lady Luck, after the nation-wide crackdown on gambling shuttered their palatial Monte Carlos in New Jersey, just across the Hudson River from Manhattan, as well as in the suburbs of half a dozen other big cities.

Their inaugural flight took place early last year and subsequent tours paid off so handsomely that the special chartered planes now operate on regular schedules. At the moment, Gothamites in-the-know can spend nights at the "Sky-High" craps tables twice weekly, if their wallets can stand the strain. As this is being written, a branch service is being readied for operation out of Houston to accommodate wealthy Texas oil men. If no unforeseen bugs develop, other major coastal cities can expect the same elegant, elaborately organized service by the end of the year.

In many ways, this new twist has tremendous advantages

which the old, earth-bound floating crap games could never give a player. For example, the now outmoded operation—which used to move around from side-street hotel to midtown garage to the back of someone's restaurant—was a constant lure to the stickup mobs. They could move in on a hot game and make everyone around the table losers in a fast few minutes.

There was also no perfect guarantee that a disgruntled loser might not tip off the game to the cops, resulting in a raid equally as painful to participants.

By doing business out over the Atlantic, the "boys" have eliminated both handicaps. No hood would dare get on board and attempt a clean-up. Where's his quick get-away? He can be sure that one slip will have his unhappy hosts helping him out the door on the longest dive of his career.

The law is just about as hamstrung. As noted earlier in this report, the plane doesn't become a gambling salon until it's well out over the ocean—far beyond the territorial limits where a cop has the authority to make a pinch. If he figures to wait until the plane returns, then seize the craps table and other equipment, he's in for an even bigger disappointment.

When the night's action is over, the cheap, easily-replaced table and the rest of the rig is simply pitched out a trap door into the sea. The seats are then replaced and the company from whom the plane was chartered is none the wiser. Then it's anyone's word against another's as to what was going on way up there at 9,000 feet. If you've read your newspaper reports on gambling raids, you know exactly how tough it is to make an arrest stick if the officers on the case can't show actual evidence of gambling.

That kind of high-class seclusion and protection costs money, so the mob makes doubly sure that it takes no pikers on board. It's not unnusual for blue-ribbon players on these flights to bring $10,000 and even $20,000 along. Thus, the plane frequently is carrying close to a quarter-million in cash. And, since only the cream of the gambling crop is invited on board, their "markers" or "I.O.U.'s" are also honored. It isn't hard to see from that how the hustlers, who bank the game, figure to cut up at least a $50,000 pot every time their ship roars down the runway. You can be sure that this typical night's take exceeds by far the per flight operating cost.

With a gold mine like that, the boys naturally aren't inviting too close an inspection of their operation. Their attitude is they may be on the side of the law or just the opposite—but why rush a decision? Behind that is their realization, of course, that should they be proved legal there'd be a quick revision of the rules to change the situation.

It's ironical, however, that the issue is so clouded as of now that no one knows precisely what the score is. There seems to be no clear law which prohibits gambling, drinking or—for that matter—running a bawdy house up in the deep blue yonder. The CAB has never had a test case which even decides who owns the air above the U.S.A., and it's a cinch that no one does out over the Atlantic or Pacific.

Just how involved the question of jurisdiction over the use of air space can get was dramatized quite a while back when Capitol Airlines brought a complaint against Northwest Airlines. Like all overseas carriers, Northwest has bars in its planes for transocean passengers to enjoy. There has never been any argument about a guy or gal's rights to imbibe out over the high seas, nor any debate on an airline's right to serve up the grog. Northwest was a unique issue because its planes travel from New York to Tokyo with a good part of that distance over the United States, and large chunks of it over states which are bone dry.

Capitol Airlines protested that the high-flying saloons should be shuttered. It argued they lacked individual licenses for each state crossed, such as trains must have for their rolling bars. The plaintiff also complained that the stratospheric bars ought to be locked while planes were flying over states where citizens on the ground couldn't legally wet their whistles. The CAB refused to rule in the case, declaring it lacked jurisdiction.

Privately, members of the board have predicted that any state in the union which tries to get authority over the ozone above it would lose its case. Thus there's a distinct chance that—for a while at least—the "Sky-High" Club is as legal as a lunchroom in Times Square.

The Broadway gamblers aren't taking any chances, however. Until now, they've avoided the spotlight by handling their games as quietly as though they were smuggling A-bombs.

You can't blame them. Theirs is one sweet racket where not only the altitude is breathtaking—

So are the profits!

Ghouls in the Morgue . . .

BLACK MARKET
IN HUMAN EYES

Corneal transplants are the modern surgical miracle for the blind, but a tragic shortage in human eyes has brought the chiselers swarming in to steal them—for a price!

IF YOU THINK money isn't everything, brother, you haven't been to New York. Money madness is master of Manhattan, and a well-stuffed wallet will get you anywhere you want to go. A crisp bill gets you the front table at a strip show when the headwaiter has already assured you that all

22

the good tables are gone. And a few more bills will get you the stripper for the evening.

But that's not all. You can buy anything in Gotham, anything at all.

Even your eyesight.

There's an old saying used to describe the utterly depraved —low enough to steal the pennies from a dead man's eyes. But modern crooks have made this ancient adage as mild as soft soap. Now they're stealing the eyes themselves!

The corneal transplant—a surgical miracle which restores vision to some of the blind—has created a frantic demand for human eyes. But medical problems and antiquated legal statutes have made it literally impossible for all who could benefit to enjoy the blessing of restored eyesight. The result is the same as it would be in anything else where an urgent need cannot be legally supplied.

So, in step the black market boys.

At the present, if an accident or disease should leave you with certain types of blindness, there's a way out of your life of total darkness—provided you have plenty of cash. Let's follow the history of a typical case in which only under-the-table payoffs wiped the shadows from a wealthy man's sight.

Our victim went duck hunting and carelessly stuck the muzzle of his shotgun in the mud. Minutes later he trained his sights on a mallard, pulled the trigger, and woke up in the hospital. He demanded the explanation for his heavily bandaged eyes and got it straight from the shoulder—he was totally blind.

Fortunately, however, the specialist who gave him the bad news was able to hold out some hope. It so happened he was suffering from damaged corneas—the transparent tissue over the irises and pupils of the eyes. Sometimes an accident, such as that gun blast, or an illness causes the clear corneas to cloud over, become foggy as milk glass. Until recently, the patient might as well have had no eyes—the effect was hopeless and permanent.

Today, surgery borrows from the dead to perform a wonder of the operating table—complete restoration of sight. The opaque corneas are removed and clear tissues are grafted in place. Recent figures show that the operation is successful in better than 89 percent of the cases of damaged corneas.

On learning about his condition, the wealthy patient waved a commanding hand and demanded, "Let's get on with it, schedule the operation for next week, if possible."

It's at this point that he and thousands of other blind persons have gotten rude shocks. They discover the problem isn't in the operation itself; there are many competent surgeons who can perform corneal grafts. The major stumbling block is getting the eyes from which the tissue can be transplanted.

Not too long ago, an organization called the *Eye Bank for Sight Restoration* set about to eliminate this problem by setting up a system of collecting eyes from persons who were willing to give, after their own death, sight to someone else. Created as a non-profit organization, the Eye Bank supplies corneal tissues to all who need and can use it, absolutely without cost. Its humanitarian principles are emphasized by the outstanding public servants on its board of directors who unselfishly devote time and energy to its worthy cause.

From the beginning, however, it fought a bitter battle with political and religious groups which denounced the operations, on grounds they were desecrations of the dead. In many states it's been only in the last six to ten years that such a transplant was possible at all, and then only where the deceased person left instructions or his next of kin gave permission for his eyes to be used in restoring sight.

That important restriction—written consent—has created the impasse which in turn created the black market. For, in strictest terms, the Eye Bank is no bank at all. Its precious assets must be used almost immediately—authorities say within nine to thirty-six hours after death of the donor—or they are worthless.

Many persons have made the mistake of contributing to the Eye Bank in their wills. That's a gift more taunting than valuable, since their bequest is often undiscovered until their funerals are over and the wills read. Others have signed special forms, available through the Eye Bank, indicating their wish to contribute their eyes. Even this doesn't always help, because the donor must die in one of those hospitals which cooperate with the bank and are familiar with its procedure. In some cases, even these hospitals learn too late of the dead patient's desires.

The result of this hopeless tangle is a long waiting list of blind persons who could and eventually will have their sight restored—if their hope lasts and they have the money or ability to get along until the operation can be performed.

First placed on a crowded waiting list, the average blind patient must wait until his name creeps toward the top. Then he's notified to stay by a telephone at all times, ready to rush to the hospital. If needed, the Red Cross provides emergency ambulance service.

That, of course, is how it goes if the unlucky blind person is poor.

Let's turn back to our sightless victim once more, to see

how it works when money is no object. His doctor lets it be known through the grapevine that a pair of eyes is desperately needed. The word whispers along the corridors of hospitals where autopsies are being performed on derelicts or the destitute and, if necessary, even the city morgue. Since his checkbook can't feel any pain, he will have his sight restored in less than four weeks after his accident—thanks to the black market.

He pays handsomely for his preferential treatment, of course. We went shopping, first for a legal and then for an illegal "speed-is-everything" operation. By cooperating with the Eye Bank, we discovered that our "blind cousin" could have the cornea transplant but he would have to wait his turn which could take years. The price is as little as $250 to $500. The top price, on this legitimate basis, was $750.

But when less scrupulous channels were checked, with price no object, a miraculous change took place. The waiting time was immediately cut in exact proportion to the increased fee. The operation could be performed in ten days, whereas normally it could have taken at least two years. Obviously, the eyes would be made available by morgue bandits. This is the black market in action.

Contrary to the layman's assumption, removing a dead person's eyes is not only comparatively simple, but can be done in a matter of minutes—often while the body still lies in the hospital bed where death took place.

Unethical doctors, internes and morgue attendants who illicitly remove eyes from the dead always have on hand glass eyes to immediately replace those stolen. Under normal circumstances, the whole thing's fool-proof. Who's going to pry open the dead man's eyes later? Even if that's done, a quick look might not reveal the substitution.

But sooner or later all thieves get caught, and that's what's been happening to these ghouls. Acting on complaints from relatives and undertakers, authorities have launched a sweeping probe into what may become one of the greatest medical scandals in modern history.

This investigation revealed the horrifying fact that in the space of one year there had been literally hundreds of illegal eye removals from deceased persons without written consent or authorization.

The probe, far from remedying this unsavory situation, has only served to make the eye pirates more wary. The vicious racket still flourishes; the black market in human eyes continues. Nothing has changed except the price, and that's sky rocketing!

But—like we said before—if you have enough money you can buy anything in Gotham . . . even your eyesight.

So, in step the black market boys.

Dial for Pleasure . . .

GOTHAM'S NO.1 MADAME

The reigning queen of the Big Town's scarlet sisterhood is not lily-white, natch. Fact is, she's a coffee-colored cutie from Lenox Avenue.

Polly Adler waved goodbye to New York fifteen years ago. The country's most famous madame, whose establishment was once the leading brokerage house in Manhattan's Stock Exchange of Sex, is retired in California. Retired too are her less-celebrated sister-madames, whose houses weren't so swank, but who offered their lusty customers plenty of action at lower prices.

Also faded into nostalgic memory is the cheery cabbie who'd sooner turn in his hack license than flunk out at providing a fare with a five-spot's worth of temporary bliss.

Gone, in New York, along with the madames and their houses, is the department store brand of sex, with a scarlet sister priced for any wallet. Bargain basement love in Gotham is a thing of the past. It has as much chance of returning as those other relics, the good five-cent cigar and the nickel subway ride.

Today's sex is sex at a price. It is frequently dispensed by the model you admired on the cover of that magazine, or the pretty young actress with the one-line walk-on role, or the haughty showgirl who wears little beside her alabaster skin. Or, just as likely, by a frisky blueblood who's doing some selling that'll never be rung up in the social register.

And the madame who supplies these svelte beauties for rent is—believe it or not—a gal who worked her way up by working her way down from Harlem's Lenox Avenue to Gotham's Park Avenue.

This dusky madame, the color of mocha with a dash of cream, is the queen of Manhattan's call girls. Her stable of fillies is strictly Caucasian however, and are the choice paymates for the big town's wine buyers and wolves.

An ardent gent could stand on the corner of 59th Street and Fifth Avenue for hours, just waiting for romance to crook a finger—and get no action, when all the while dozens of luscious squabs are on call within walking distance.

But you'd have to know where to call. To connect with one of these dolls, all you've got to do is dig a dime from your pocket—and Madame Mocha's number from your little black book. This mother hen of beautiful chicks has adapted one of the gimmicks of streamlined New York, the answering service, to make her operation safe from snooping cops and blackmailing hoods.

The hallmark of Polly Adler was her house that was not a home. This dusky successor to the Adler throne has a home in the East 50's—but it's not a house.

A bordello in New York is as out of style as five dollars worth of love. But if you've got madame's number, your love comes to you, as tastefully packaged as if she came from the pages of a top fashion magazine.

You can talk about the good old days, but La Adler's house was just plain old-fashioned. Her whole girly operation belonged back with the Model T. Polly had her problems. Her sporting palace was a sitting duck for the police. The premises could be raided, the phones tapped, the play-for-pay girls nabbed. You can't just toss all that into a satchel and steal away into the night.

Despite the payoffs, despite precautions, the country's most famous —and most literary—madame was constantly plagued by the law; and although she was never convicted of any serious charges, popping in and out of police stations and courtrooms is rough on a girl who's trying to run a business.

If Polly were to leave California, where she's soaking up sunshine and culture, to take a look at the professional game of love as played by today's reigning madame, she would never recognize it.

Madame Mocha's transactions in flesh are as modern as the Park Avenue steel and glass towers that replaced the ornate brownstones of Polly Adler's day.

Madame Mocha has no house; she uses no phones that can

be tapped; she has no chippies sitting around waiting for action. All she has is an answering service.

And the lonely guy, in the market for love, needs only a ten-cent piece and Madame's phone number.

But even with the number, you can't call her—she calls you. All you do is leave your number with her answering service. She returns your call, but from a public telephone and thus she enjoys that good feeling of knowing she's not being bugged.

If she knows you, or if you've been well-recommended, she'll drop another dime in the slot and call one of her pigeons. Before you have a chance to mix a couple of martinis and smooth down the covers, there'll be a package from Madame delivered to your door . . . and her goods are the best in town.

The dime for your phone call is the last bargain you'll be getting in this love-for-sale. The mocha madame's introduction charge is twenty-five dollars and on top of this you pay the tab for the cutie. That's between you and the babe.

Then if you like the dolls, and it's hard not to, the madame stays out of it. From then on you make your own arrangements.

Unlike her predecessors, Madame Mocha does not share in her girl's take. That's why they like her. But anytime you call her for new talent, there's that twenty-five dollar introduction fee.

The beauts in her stable don't think twice about Madame's shade. It's a case of economic benefit breaking down the color barrier. It's the Brotherhood of the Buck.

Does Madame Mocha ring a familiar bell? Well, if you've been to some of the usual Park Avenue wingdings, you've probably run into her. She's short, curvaceous and exotic looking, and she's all business. She's like the bartender who never touches the stuff. She's in the business, but he doesn't indulge. Her clientele knows there's no action as far as she's concerned.

But if your wallet is filled, and you've got the right number, just spin the dial if you want to play Romeo to a willing Juliet right in your own parlor.

With Mickey Jelke out of sight and Polly Adler in California since 1945, Madame Mocha rules the roost. Her naughty racket is streamlined, raid-proof and tap-proof . . . and, except for her, it's lily-white. But it's sure not 99 and 44-one hundreths percent pure.

BUNDLE OF DREAMS IN LOCKER 787

The dope hustler has a brand new dodge to duck the cops. He's not peddling drugs, he's selling keys!

Along NEW YORK's Tenderloin, they're selling keys for twenty-five dollars and up. On 42nd Street between Seventh and Eighth Avenues, little men in doorways exchange the keys for plenty of folding green. On Dream Street—that blaring block of 47th Street between Sixth and Seventh—

the keys pass from hand to hand—and so does the cabbage.

On the corner of Seventh Avenue and Fiftieth, where the hustlers go hip-swinging and the pimps go pandering, still more of the expensive keys are for sale.

They aren't made of gold or platinum. They won't open the door of the apartment of some voluptuous vixen. But a guy with a monkey on his back can open the door to his dreams and pass through the portals of Paradise if he's got the price of a key.

This game of Hide-The-Keys is as simple as it is slick. It's the latest scheme for pushing dope under the eyes of the law, and it's so smooth that it's giving the Narcotics Squad a headache all the aspirin in the world couldn't cope with.

The cardinal rule among dope peddlers for years has been, simply stated, "Don't get nailed with the goods." Knowing a guy is a pusher won't put him behind bars; you have to put the finger on him while the stuff is still in his possession. This stacks the deck for the dope dealers, but with state, local and federal authorities tightening the noose along Manhattan's hardened artery, pushers have been finding it increasingly difficult to stay out of the net.

Narcotics is a racket where the profits are staggering. There's never been a shortage of pushers willing to take the risk, but the rats who feed on the twitching addicts are always looking for a little of the best of it. Now they've come up with a switch that's got the law turned upside-down.

How does the dope hustler do it? Simple. Manhattan has public lockers by the thousands. You'll find them in the 42nd Street IRT subway station in a dozen different locations. Ditto for Penn Station, Grand Central and most large bus depots in the midtown area. The same goes for the airline terminals.

They're innocent and necessary public conveniences, and

you've probably used them yourself. When a peddler makes his connection for a "buy" of heroin, he takes the stuff and wraps it up in assorted little packages. The amount of "H" in the package regulates the price.

The crafty peddler goes to various spots in the city where the lockers are located. He deposits a package in the box and locks it with a key that costs from a dime to a quarter. There is a number on the key that corresponds with the number on the locker. He will stash a half-dozen packages that vary in price in lockers in six different locations.

Now the pusher is clean, without a shred of junk on him. All he has is a pocketful of keys, but for the poor wretches he's servicing, he's carrying a pocketful of dreams.

When the rat who peddles kicks by the ounce finally makes contact with the addict, the only exchange between them is money and a key. No dope changes hands—and without dope there is no evidence for a pinch. Thus the law can't put the collar on him. With thousands of lockers spread all over the city, it is virtually impossible for the cops to keep an eye on all of them.

The dream merchant sells the deadly stuff by remote control. The addict pays the going price and gets a key with a number on it. Then the frantic junkie makes a bee-line for the locker, knowing that within the hour he'll be shaking that monkey off his back.

This new system of drops for dope delivery is almost like having a bunch of little stores all over town. And business has been very good, much to the chagrin of the eagle-eyed narcotic dicks.

So the next time you lift a parcel out of one of these lockers, remember that it might have held a different kind of package a few hours before—a package full of dreams.

Operation Diaper . . .

CALL 'EM DADDY

Here's how any man can find himself an innocent victim of the tender trap. This latest gimmick of the Broadway chippies is the scandal of New York's paternity courts.

YES—IT COULD happen to *you* in New York. It could happen to you—*even if you are absolutely innocent!*

Let's try to picture the scene. It takes place in a New York courtroom six months from now. There, on the witness stand, is Shiela—the girl your office hired for a brief period a couple of years ago to do secretarial work. You never heard of her or saw her again until a few months ago—when the men from the Detective squad came and threw you in jail!

To your astonishment, you find that Shiela has named *you* as the father of her out-of-wedlock child!

Into jail you went. Then you had to raise $500 bail your-self—in cash—because no bail bond company will post bond in a paternity suit. Only then were you released and given a chance to talk with a lawyer.

Then came more shocks. You told your lawyer the truth —that you are absolutely innocent. To your astonishment, the lawyer advised you to yield to blackmail—*to pay the girl off rather than to fight the case in court!*

You could hardly believe your ears. But the lawyer ex-plained why. Every year the courts of the City of New York convict hundreds of innocent men on paternity charges. Ac-cording to the law the girl who accuses you needs no evidence of any kind, other than her own word, to win her case. Men are frequently convicted on less than five minutes' unsubstan-tiated testimony by the accusing female, and are required by the court to make payments for a period of sixteen years, totaling $10,000 or more!

"But what about a blood test?" you asked. "Since I'm in-nocent, won't that prove it?"

It might, the lawyer explained—but then again, it might not. Modern blood tests can clear only about half of all in-nocent men. The other half are victims of coincidence—they have elements in their blood that are the same as the elements in the child's blood. It doesn't prove that they are the father of the child—it's all a matter of coincidence and chance.

"The trouble is," said your lawyer, "if the blood test doesn't absolutely clear you, many judges simply assume that you are

37

the guy who did it. They hardly consider the testimony. And not only that—your business friends, and your personal friends, also believe that you are guilty. I've seen many an innocent man ruined personally and professionally, for life, on a paternity rap, when they were absolutely innocent."

"You mean to say," you asked, "that this little floozy can convict me on her own word only?"

"She certainly can," your lawyer said. "I'd advise you to avoid the whole mess, and avoid all the publicity too, by paying her off. It's easier to convict a man on a paternity rap in New York City than it is to convict him of a ten dollar traffic violation!"

Well, you decided *not* to yield to blackmail. You decided to fight for justice in court. You had bad luck on the blood test—you were among the 50% of innocent men whose innocence was *not* established by the test. That is, you had elements in your blood that are also present in the child's blood. And now, there is Shiela on the witness stand, telling a fantastic story of nights with you in her apartment—every word false.

And you are convicted! The judge requires you to pay Shiela $75 a month for sixteen years!

Sound too fantastic to be true?

Unfortunately the truth about Operation Diaper is stranger —and more shocking—than fiction. At this very writing, scores of girls are flocking into the New York courts to pin paternity raps on innocent men. In untold numbers of other cases, the man takes his lawyer's advice and pays the wench off rather than go through the ordeal of public humiliation, family disaster, and possible professional ruin—that a paternity action can bring.

The chippies know that the law is lax—and they are making

the most of it. They choose their victims carefully—decent family men who simply can't face or can't afford such scandal. These are the soft touches—the suckers who come through with as much as $5,000 or $10,000 as soon as the girl threatens to make her accusation public.

The incredible story of Operation Diaper is now coming to light. Recent blood test results have been carefully studied, and improvements in techniques of blood testing have been clearing more and more innocent men—although a lot of men continue to be the victims of coincidence and chance.

Recently Sidney B. Schatkin, former Assistant Corporation Counsel of the City of New York, and Dr. Leon B. Sussman, one of the nation's foremost authorities on blood testing, wrote an article on the results of studies they had made of 4,000 cases in which men had been convicted on paternity raps in New York courts.

They found that, out of the 4,000 men convicted in one year, at least 850 were absolutely and unquestionably innocent! Schatkin and Sussman pointed out that their survey did not even include the thousands of innocent victims who paid off as soon as the accusation was made—without even bothering to fight it in court.

Schatkin is probably the world's leading authority on paternity suits. For 28 years he handled paternity actions for the City of New York, and now he is in private practice. His clients include many of the rich and famous men of America, who come to him for his expert advice when they get in trouble.

In recent statements, Schatkin has gone even beyond the unbelievable revelations in his article in the *Law Journal*. He has revealed that, in 30% to 40% of *all* paternity accusations, the girls are accusing innocent men! No other field of law in America, says Schatkin, is so full of perjury, blackmail, and fraud.

He blames the mess on our antiquated laws—and on the smart dames who have learned how to take advantage of them. In New York City, he points out, any man can be thrown in jail the moment a woman accuses him. This alone is enough to make many innocent men want to settle the whole thing by paying off, rather than have her file formal charges.

And then there is the problem of evidence. The cutie doesn't need any to convict you! This is true in almost every state in the Union.

As a matter of fact, New York is the only state in which there has even been some attempt to correct this defect in the law. In 1952 the late New York State Assemblyman Bernard Austin, who had studied the problem and become indignant at the racket that many girls were operating at the expense of decent men, introduced a bill in the State Legislature requiring some evidence other than the girl's word in order to convict a man in a paternity suit. No sooner had he introduced it than several legislators jumped to their feet.

"A blow to womanhood!" one of them yelled.

The bill was defeated and was never reintroduced. So men in New York City are right back where they started from— at the mercy of the chippie who decides to pick them as the next victim in Operation Diaper.

The unfair laws governing our paternity courts reflect our history and also our country's social attitudes. Remember that blood testing is a recent development, and that women have been accusing innocent men from time immemorial. Before the days of blood testing the courts had no really convincing proof of *anybody's* innocence.

Frequently, the courts would simply throw up their hands

at the torrent of lies and counter-lies that often surrounded paternity suits. They took the easy way out—that is, they simply convicted any man that a wench dragged into court.

Blood tests represent a great step forward. Half of all genuinely innocent men can have their innocence scientifically proven by blood tests. The analysis of the girl's blood, her child's blood, and the blood of the man she accuses, shows that the child has elements in his blood that aren't present in either the mother's blood or the blood of the man she is accusing. Obviously, then, those elements came from the *real* father— the man who really conceived the child—and not from the man the mother is trying to pin the rap on.

Courts, unfortunately, have been slow in accepting the absolute proofs of modern science. In many states in the Union, the court is still free to convict a man who has been excluded by the blood test and therefore has been scientifically proven innocent!

This, fortunately, is one hazard that an accused man in New York City does not face. In 1935 the legislature passed a law that requires courts to accept unchallenged scientific blood test results excluding the accused man as absolute proof of his innocence. But this represents only a bare beginning toward ending Operation Diaper, a racket that is soaring in New York today rather than diminishing.

Much of the racket depends on the success of blackmail threats. The unwed mother chooses a man who she knows will do everything possible to avoid the scandal and publicity of a paternity suit—and that includes most men. She first approaches him informally and tells him that she would be willing to let the whole thing drop if he will pay her, say, $10,000.

The man is in a dilemma. In such cases the babe will of course refuse a voluntary blood test, and therefore the man has no idea whether or not he falls in the lucky 50% of innocent men whose innocence is demonstrated by such tests. The only way he can find this out is to let the girl go ahead and file her charges, and then have the court order blood tests of the mother, child, and himself.

But this brings an immediate storm of publicity—the very thing the man wants to avoid at all costs. If he is at all prominent, he will be personally dragged through the front pages of the newspapers that thrive on such stories. Many or most people are willing to assume that he is the father—or at least that he has been having a torrid affair with the cutie—no matter *what* the blood tests show.

For this reason the blackmailing females often choose married men who are respected figures. They know they can wreck such individuals *just by filing the charges!*

Few such men are prepared to face the effects that the charges and the immediate scandalous publicity will have on their families, their children, and of course their business careers. They go into a quick huddle with their lawyers, and, after finding out the shocking facts of the way in which paternity courts convict innocent men, decide not to fight. They pay.

The racket works so well that some women have become incredibly bold. Schatkin tells the story of one of America's best-known entertainers, whose name he carefully conceals. Lets call him Fred Famous. He has a contract that guarantees him a tremendous annual income for a long period of years. Now this contract, like all such contracts, has a morals clause. It provides that his salary can be cancelled if the entertainer creates a public scandal. The clause, of course, makes good sense.

Unfortunately, it also puts Fred Famous, and other well-known entertainment personalities, at the mercy of Operation Diaper.

Most of New York's scheming sisterhood know about the morals clauses in the contracts of big-name entertainers. These girls look on the clauses as almost a kind of insurance for them. If they get pregnant and have a baby, they simply pick out one of the "big boys" and threaten to start a paternity suit against him unless he agrees to pay off. And of course the resulting scandal could cause a lucrative contract to be terminated.

That's what happened to Fred Famous. A playgirl, well known around the nightspots, had a child and quietly contacted Fred Famous, whom she barely knew. She, of course, refused to accede voluntarily to a blood test—she simply told Famous that if he did not promptly start paying her $600 a month she would start a paternity suit against him.

Famous was on the spot. He could obtain a court-ordered blood test only *after* she filed the suit. But by then the big scandal would have been launched. The test, obtained at such risk to his professional status, would give him only a 50-50 chance of demonstrating his innocence. And if it didn't exclude him, it was all too likely that a conviction in court would follow, resulting in the almost certain loss of his contract. He thought it over, and agreed to pay if she would agree not to file the suit.

This went on for several years; then the play girl got even bolder. She went to Famous again, and told him that she was having a little trouble living on $600 a month. She wanted $1,000 a month.

"Think it over, Fred," she said coolly. "It's worth it to you to pay me one thousand dollars monthly and protect what you have. If you fight, you'll probably lose everything."

Now she gets $1,000 a month. Unbelievable? Absolutely not! This is an actual case—one of hundreds where much lesser personalities are involved.

The rate of illegitimate births has tripled in the last two decades. In New York City the number of paternity suits has more than doubled in six years. Fraud and blackmail are rampant.

If you are a playboy—you may be next. And if you *aren't* a playboy—you *still* may be next.

Until our laws are changed, and until there is a large-scale crackdown on perjury and fraud in our paternity courts, Operation Diaper is going to continue as one of the biggest and most lucrative rackets ever dreamed up to take advantage of "the tender trap."

Minx and Minks . . .

THE MINK COAT RACKET

Known by the cocktail set as the "mink switch," here is low larceny as it is being practiced by high society!

ONE OF THESE nights, when you've got money to burn and the urge to burn it, take yourself over to one of the ultra chic East Side niteries. El Morocco, say, or the Colony, or any of the plush palaces where the lighting is subtle, the service silent, and the clientele smells of money.

Take a look at the lovelies scattered around the room. They're powdered and pampered and perfumed. Their dialogue is crisp and polished and their seams are always straight . . . but sometimes their ideas are not. Just ask one of them what they'd do for a mink coat.

But don't put that same question to the nation's big insurance companies these days. They're tearing their hair out over a fresh swindle that's practically foolproof, mainly because it's *not* being worked by the crowd that practices larceny full time. Instead, the gimmick is used by otherwise highly respectable matrons who don't mind dabbling in a swindle—just once when the pay-off's in brand new furs.

The stunt, itself, is disarmingly simple. Take, for example, the wife of a successful business man living in a New York suburb. Let's call her Mrs. X. She and her husband own their own home, have a comfortable bank balance and are pillars of their community. The only cloud on her horizon is her three-year-old mink. She'd like a *new* one—but hubby has put his foot down.

It looks hopeless, until she gets the whisper from a friend during an afternoon bridge session. If she has insurance, there *is* a way to get a new coat—and for free. And hubby needn't suspect a thing.

Naturally, Mrs. X *does* have insurance on her mink. There are a lot of professions in which a woman simply can't buy insurance on jewels, furs and other valuables—show business is one of them. Too risky. Not in this case, though. The company is only too willing to write a policy for someone with her excellent background.

That sets the scene for one of the slickest dodges ever to come from putting two curly heads together. Mrs. X carefully picks a night when she and her husband are to dine in town with a group of long-time friends, and whispers to her confederate the details of where they'll be—and when.

Upon entering the cafe, night club or hotel dining room, she leaves her mink in the checkroom and gets the usual stub for it. Later, her co-conspirator enters with her escort and settles at the bar for a few drinks. She checks her coat, too, but it's a comparatively inexpensive mink-dyed muskrat—with all labels and identification removed.

Following a strict timetable, the two meet in the ladies room and casually switch coat checks right under the nose of the un-suspecting powder room attendant. Both return to their places and, shortly thereafter, the artful wench at the bar leaves with her companion—but *not* wearing the muskrat she arrived in.

Instead, she uses her switched coat check and departs swathed in mink. The harried hat check girl doesn't even pause in giving the woman what her check calls for.

But the air in the place turns blue an hour later when Mrs. X presents *her* check and is handed a muskrat worth only a frac-tion of her mink. The management is called instantly. Stand-ing around her are a genuinely outraged husband and her friends—all of them ready to swear she left a mink coat in the checkroom.

The discussion with the hotel or restaurant representa-tive is brief. He wants to settle as quietly and amicably as pos-sible. He can't afford to offend such patrons. Besides, he's insured too.

Now it's up to the insurance companies and eventually Mrs. X gets the big pay-off from her policy—enough to get that brand new mink.

Her accomplice? She's wearing mink, too, the one she so deftly picked up in the restaurant.

And it's as neat as it is naughty. What, if by some very re-

47

mote chance, the two women are caught at it? They merely exchange coats and there are apologies all around for the regrettable mistake. No one would think of crying thief at such reputable ladies.

As for the insurance company, it has three things:

(1) An unclaimed muskrat.

(2) A headache in the growing list of ultra-respectable matrons who are pulling this new confidence game.

(3) Another proof of the age-old fact that there seems to be a little larceny in even the *nicest* people.

Vest-pocket killer . . .

SHOT AND KILLED BY
A RONSON LIGHTER!

Sound ridiculous? You won't think so after reading this report, showing how harmless cigarette lighters are being turned into deadly weapons!

Two SQUAD CARS of police had raced into a tenement district to break up a rumble between rival gangs of young, tough hoodlums. Having averted the pitched battle, the cops lined the boys against a wall and made the usual frisk for zip guns, switchblade knives and similar weapons.

49

One cop was automatically handing cigarettes and a lighter back to a tough he'd searched thoroughly when the policeman's hand stopped in mid-air.

There was nothing wrong with the cigarettes. But the lighter hefted like it was full of lead, far too heavy for the job it had originally been constructed to do. And a quick inspection under the street lights brought confirmation of the cop's suspicions.

Once an inexpensive, stock model Ronson, it had been converted into a vest pocket pistol. And the grim truth is that more than a few slayings may eventually be linked to this miniature murder weapon.

For beyond turning up the fact of its existence, the subsequent investigation also revealed that exact blueprints for the construction of this innocent looking killer have been peddled all over the country—for one dollar each—by a New York firm operating from hole-in-the-wall offices not far from the heart of Times Square.

With the plans in hand, making a "lighter gun" is entirely *too* simple for such artful minds as the teen-age inventors of zip guns and other homemade death-dealers. The major item is an ordinary "push down" type of lighter, such as the Ronson or other similar makes.

The top assembly is removed and—in place of the wick holder—a tube of brass or hard steel is inserted, running from the bottom to the cap of the lighter. Then the cotton is removed from the fluid compartment which is filled with molten lead and allowed to harden.

The "trigger" on this pint-sized passport to eternity is a piece of spring steel, welded to the bottom on one end. At the other end of the steel piece is a firing pin made of a machine screw which has been filed to a sharp point.

With the top replaced, it looks like any other lighter, at a casual glance. Now, however, it is a murder weapon.

The brass or steel tube is a snug fit for a .22 short bullet— plenty good enough to kill. To use the "gun," its operator flips the cap up just as you would if you were getting a light. With his thumb, he pulls back the spring steel "trigger" and lets go.

What is particularly alarming is that the contraption is so innocent looking. An officer searching a shooting suspect could easily hand him back his cigarettes and "lighter" and be unaware they were returning the very thing they were hunting for.

But a smart cop who's onto this new gimmick can spot one of the converted lighters easily by the fact that it's suspiciously heavy—due to the lead in it—and by the firing mechanism which protrudes slightly beyond the bottom.

How many blueprints of this cigarette "lighter gun" have been distributed is anyone's guess, but they undoubtedly number in the thousands.

Cops approaching and searching hoodlums will do well to bear one thing in mind.

Make sure your next light isn't your last.

The sign says "GENTLEMEN."
But it should say . . .

BEWARE THE
HOMO FRAME-UP

Every man who walks into an unattended public rest room is a potential victim!

THE SIGN ON the door gave no hint that the professor was about to enter one of the local branches of a "business" that has grown to frightening proportions. Neither did the fixtures inside suggest that here was a place where big "deals" often begin.

The sign, a single commonplace word, said tersely GENTLE-MEN. The fixtures were just what any man would expect to find in a public lavatory. But before the professor left he found himself committed to the most costly purchase he had ever made.

The commodity he bought was "silence." He paid for it, not because he was guilty of any offense, but because the mere accusation is more than most men dare to face. To an instructor in a boys' prep school, the charge, whether proved or not, was loaded with the kind of dynamite that would put an end to his career.

The unfortunate professor was another innocent victim of the "Homo Frame-up," to call it by the ugly label the punks of the underworld have given to an ugly racket.

Originally, the "Homo Frame-up" was exactly what the name suggests, a blackmail trap set for known homosexuals. It was a soft racket and a safe one; the pervert was in no position to complain to the law. He was obviously guilty and the only thing he could do was pay if he wanted to avoid exposure.

Then some shabby shakedown artist figured out that the crooked frame might just as successfully be hung on victims who weren't homos—men who, for the very reason that they were *not* perverts, would be doubly anxious to avoid any hint of homosexual practices.

The result is a racket that is enriching its organizers and enraging law enforcement officers. There are many variations of the scheme, but the way it was worked on the professor is typical.

A few seconds after the professor entered the deserted men's room in a Broadway subway station, a pale young man followed him through the door. The professor noted immediately that the boy standing beside him looked quite ill. He seemed to be swaying on his feet, then he gasped, his legs buckled, and he slumped toward the professor, who managed to catch him in time to save him from crashing to the tiled floor.

It was at this exact moment that the two "detectives" walked in. This split-second timing was no accident. They were not in any way connected with the police. They were members of the blackmail team and their crooked play had been practiced to a count in the same way a well-drilled football team runs off its formations. They always managed to arrive at the most compromising moment, and their outspoken version of what they saw did not bother to mince four-letter words.

In horrified disbelief, the professor heard the young man, an obvious deviate, profess his own innocence while he accused the professor of making advances. In reply to the frantic professor's attempts to explain, the pseudo-detectives grimly told him he'd have to "Tell it to the judge."

Fearful of harmful publicity, this was exactly what the professor couldn't afford to do. Trapped by the embarrassing circumstances, the panic-stricken victim never thought to ask the fake detectives to show credentials; never wondered how the more sympathetic of the pair managed to dissuade his tough-sounding partner from taking him right down to headquarters.

It cost the professor all the cash he had with him and a promise of more to follow. He might still be meeting their extortion demands but for a lucky break. One morning, more than a year after he had been trapped, he opened his newspaper and saw the pictures of two faces that had become all too familiar. The caption beneath said, "*Convicted of impersonating officers of the law.*"

It seldom ends that way, because police officials are help-less, since innocent victims of this slimy racket hesitate to co-operate.

In the case reported in the newspaper, the mark was trapped in a motion picture theater near one of the city's leading boys' schools. This is another of the hunting grounds for these mongrels of the underworld.

But the gangs aren't choosey. They don't prey only on specially selected prizes. *Every lone man who walks into an unattended public lavatory is a potential target for the "Homo Frame-up."* If he is unfortunate enough to choose the wrong place at the right time.

Top law enforcement officials know that the few cases that ever come to trial are, like the iceberg, only the surface indi-cations of a city-wide menace. What makes them especially bitter about the success of this foul racket is that the rat in every successful shakedown of this kind *is posing as a crooked cop*.

It's a vicious circle, a ride to hell and back on the subway express. The louse gets away with impersonating an officer, and the pervert who acted as the come-on usually goes free. All because the victim pays and rarely squawks.

So, though the story is distasteful, here it is.

Your best protection against the underground "Homo Frame-up" is knowing how it works. When you ride the sub-way, make sure they don't take *you* for a ride.

Taking the heat off "hot" money . . .

THE SWISS SWITCH

That's what the silk-lined mobocracy calls the latest scheme to turn dishonest dollars into honest dollars without paying Uncle Sam's tax bite!

IF UNCLE SAM'S REVENUE men want to uncover the biggest tax leak of all time, they'd better start climbing the Alps. Because the answer is way over in Switzerland.

The scheme was blueprinted by the multi-million dollar empire of crime that made rich New York its own personal melon. The silk-lined ace hoodlums had to find a way to surface the "hot" money they are taking out of New York's lush narcotics industry, numbers racket and every other form of illegitimate enterprise.

The loot from these operations is valueless unless it can be accounted for to the satisfaction of the U.S. Internal Revenue Department. So, New York's gang overlords, with the connivance of astute lawyers and accountants, developed what they call the "Swiss Switch," one of the smoothest schemes ever devised to legitimatize their illegitimate cash and do Uncle Whiskers out of his tax bite.

Payment on many millions of dollars is being evaded by the underworld's tax dodgers with the aid and encouragement of certain Swiss banks. Already among the richest in the world, these institutions have become bursting warehouses of undeclared cash, siphoned from the proceeds of underworld rackets.

The Geneva banks openly boast that depositors are shielded from prying Revenue men of other lands, by these special laws which shroud all Swiss bank dealings in secrecy.

The high echelon hoods, eager to cheat on their Federal and State income tax returns, are assured that officers and employees of Swiss banks, seeking their patronage, will never reveal their dealings to anybody. By Swiss law, the bank employee who violates such a confidence is subject to fine and imprisonment.

Tax dodgers, desiring super-secrecy, are provided with accounts which they can manipulate, by signing Swiss bank deposit and withdrawal slips with *a number instead of a name*— thus enabling a depositor to completely conceal his identity.

How does this trans-Atlantic invitation to criminals, known in the underworld as the "Swiss Switch" work? Let's suppose a racketeer finds himself with $100,000 in unreported cash. He may have won it in gambling, or in any one of a dozen illegitimate ways.

Does he have to put the money in a valise and take a plane to Switzerland? Not at all. He simply writes or cables the main office of a bank in Switzerland, which opens an account for him under a number instead of a name.

The Swiss bank's New York office is notified of the existence of the numbered account. The tax cheat can then walk in, and identify himself by writing out his number in longhand, for purposes of comparison, and carry on his business.

If United States authorities want to investigate, they cannot force the foreign bank officials to violate Swiss law by identifying the holder of account number so-and-so. Nor can they get the information from the New York branch manager because, he can honestly say that he doesn't have it.

If the cheat wants to withdraw his money all he has to do is cable Geneva through the local branch and the packet of American bank notes will be mailed to his address.

This is only the beginning.

Some of Switzerland's banks go so far as to brazenly boast that *anonymous*, yes, we said anonymous, banking service is available. This provides the perfect cover-up. They slyly promote the easy inference that a powerful foreign institution is ready and willing to help tax dodging characters circumvent U.S. laws by hiding behind Swiss laws.

So cooperative have these Swiss banks become in fomenting international chicanery, while talking piously about the "customer's" sacred rights, that the tax dodger does not have to settle for merely secreting his hoard there. The real gimmick is about to come.

The more enterprising of the Swiss bankers have devised

a neat trick, to wit: depositors are permitted to "borrow" funds against illegitimate cash on deposit in their banks. This is the ultimate refinement for the tax cheat. The racketeer's "hot" money then becomes legitimate appearing on his books as a bank loan on which he is paying normal interest rates.

For the sake of appearances, the records will show that he has pledged his business assets—usually a front for his illegitimate activities—as "collateral." In this way he has the use of hundreds of thousands of undeclared cash for any enterprise, legitimate or otherwise.

And he can live it up in his accustomed silk-lined luxury, with his broads, his Cadillacs and his penthouses, without ever disclosing where or how he got the money in the first place.

As a final ironic twist, the interest he pays to the Swiss Bank on such a "loan," is deductible from his U.S. income tax. Clever? . . . that's the "Swiss Switch!"

It is only in recent months that some of the Geneva banks began to openly court the business of Americans in the more modest income brackets. These banks have been encouraged to branch out by our continuing high tax rate and by their success over many years in handling funds for the international shady.

The latter gentry—ganglords, dethroned kings, deposed dictators and big-time swindlers, have favored the Swiss banks as havens for their illegal hoards.

Albert Anastasia, Lord High Executioner of Murder, Inc., and recently shot to death in a Manhattan barber shop, is known to have cached millions of his ill-gotten gains in a numbered account in Geneva.

Before he went into exile, ex-Dictator Juan Peron of Argentina reportedly stashed $50,000,000 in a numbered account so that his identity as a depositor could never be exposed.

"Longie" Zwillman, underworld czar of the vending machine racket, who committed suicide in the basement of his palatial home, is also said to have been a heavy depositor with a numbered account in Switzerland.

And when U.S. T-men smashed a multi-million dollar dope ring in New York last fall, they unearthed evidence that the operators maintained at least two Swiss numbered bank accounts.

It might be asked, why must an American seeking to avoid payment of income tax, bank his money in far-off Switzerland? Can't he simply put it into a safety deposit box here, dipping in for cash as needed?

He can. Many have tried it. But those who risked safe deposit boxes often found tax sleuths, armed with court order, opening them and confiscating the contents pending explanations.

Safer than a safe deposit box is the Swiss bank account which, unfortunately, T-Men cannot get at. Flaunting this fact boldly, one of the Geneva institutions points out that the Swiss franc is as strong as the dollar. It adds:

"The Swiss respect the right of the individual to keep his personal affairs secret. They have no intention of permitting the incorporation in their code of law of any false ideas of the "right" of a taxation authority to be informed of the financial situation of an individual."

Until the U.S. Government does something about this blatant sabotaging of its laws, more and more tax swindlers are going to be tempted to beat the tax by listening to the siren Swiss song. And honest taxpayers will be forced to make up the many millions that are siphoned off.

The Swiss, of course, following their own laws, are committing no crime. But the tax cheats, using Switzerland's banks and numbered accounts to evade taxes, are flirting with prison bars.

Someday, somehow, the veil of secrecy will be pierced.

When that happens, those who yielded to temptation to conceal their names, will end up with numbers . . . across their chests.

"Selling the Stiffs" . . .

THE NEW C.O.D. RACKET

When Uncle Whiskers put a crimp in the old C.O.D. dodge of grave robbing by mail, the "boys" came right back with a slick new angle . . .

Y OU CAN'T KEEP a good con man down, it seems. Let the law put the quietus on his illegal dodge for a while and he's almost sure to come up with a switcheroo that gets him back in business again—often on a sounder basis than before. And that's exactly what has happened in the case of that time-tested old swindle, the C.O.D. racket—or, as the swindlers themselves called it, "Selling the Stiffs."

Here's the way it used to work:

The grifter would consult newspaper obituary columns and draw up a huge mailing list of recently deceased persons and send a small C.O.D. package to each one of them. The charge was about $3. When the package arrived at the home of the dead person, the $3 would invariably be paid without question by some relative or friend of the family who naturally assumed it had been ordered by the dear departed.

Unfortunately, according to law, C.O.D. packages cannot be opened or inspected until after payment has been made. When the parcel was opened, it usually revealed some ten cent can opener, or comparable item of cheap merchandise.

What did the victims do about it? Usually nothing—what with the emotional strain and distress of a bereaved and often disorganized household. Which, of course, was just what the sharpshooter was counting on.

This heartless racket was finally squelched, some years back, partly as the outcome of the investigation and publicity which followed the sending of a cheap pen to a dead man, who, in his lifetime, had been unable to read or write! The end result was a new Federal regulation to the effect that no C.O.D. package could be sent without a written order.

This put the damper on the C.O.D. racket, but the hustlers didn't roll over and play dead, not by a long shot. No sir— the Badtown boys put their little pointed heads together and before you could say "shell game," they had come up with this new twist on the old gimmick.

The new-style grifter scans the death notices as before, and compiles his list of victims, but he doesn't send out a package. He's too smart for that. He sends a letter, addressed to one of the deceased listed in the obituary columns. The swindler, in this letter, says he is in the business of buying up unclaimed packages from the Post Office.

The letter goes on to say that he has in his possession a package addressed to so-and-so (the dead person). He paid a few dollars for it, he says, sight unseen, and he's willing to send it along, for what it cost him, C.O.D. of course. All the recipient has to do is drop him a postcard authorizing the C.O.D. shipment. The sharpie's letterhead always carries some legitimate-sounding handle such as, "C.O.D. Recovery Service."

It's all very cozy and safe for the con man, even though he has no such package, nor any such business. And he knows his pitch will hook the suckers nine times out of ten. Here's what happens. A widow, for instance, receives this letter—addressed to her late husband—opens it, and usually falls into the sharpshooter's trap.

She knows nothing about any package, but figures old Gus must have ordered something before he kicked the bucket, and anyway she's too upset to think straight. So she sends off a letter authorizing the crook to send the package C.O.D. He makes up a phony package and shoots it along.

When she opens the package, addressed to her late hubby, she finds a piece of junk worth a dime—and she's stuck with it. All she can do is cry. This slick gimmick is a fraud, but hanging a rap on the con man is something else again.

He has his C.O.D. "order," remember? And to give him a short haircut and a long stretch, the one who has been defrauded must testify against him. In this case the one defrauded is also departed. The widow was not defrauded, so she can't testify. In fact, she's technically guilty of opening somebody else's mail.

All in all, it's a pretty vicious racket, operated by people who have no scruples at all about taking profitable advantage of a griefstricken household.

So here's a word to the wise: If you have a death in your family and shortly after receive a letter similar to the one quoted above, turn it over to your FBI office or the postal inspectors. They'll soon find out if the deal is on the square or just the C.O.D. con man at his dirty work again.

By doing this you may play a part in helping Uncle Sam crack down on these heartless grifters. Because you can be sure Uncle's busy right now figuring some way to plug that loophole in the law that permits what amounts to a kind of legalized grave-robbing by mail.

Paging Willie Sutton . . .

HOW SAFE IS
YOUR BANK?

If you think your money is locked up tight in a bank, just ask who has a key to the front door . . . could be an ex-con with a broom!

FRED X, SING SING prison number 100,226, unlocked the steel doors of a branch of a New York bank and slipped inside. Nine hours later he emerged and hurried off into the night.

During those nine hours Fred, who had left Sing Sing only a few months before, after serving five years for armed robbery—was alone in the bank. He had access to safety deposit boxes containing fortunes in cash, jewels and bonds. A veritable arsenal of guns was within his reach. He knew how to turn off the burglar alarm. The huge vault containing its bundles of cash awaited his command.

What did ex-convict No. 100,226 do about it?

Nothing, for Fred X, late of Sing Sing Penitentiary, was the bank's official cleaning man.

Throughout New York City, other men with criminal records like Fred, each night descend on banks with mop and dustcloth—and at any moment can substitute for these humble tools, safecracking equipment and guns.

All this is made easy by unscrupulous cleaning companies who hire these men at coolie wages, only because ex-convicts can be induced to work for salaries far below the $65-a-week average for porters and janitors.

Fred often worked for as low as $35, and other men with criminal records toil for less—simply because these greedy cleaning contractors, determined to attract business away from their ethical competitors who concern themselves about the prior background of prospective employees, ask no questions in exchange for cheap labor.

Some banks, equally pleased to benefit from this substandard wage arrangement, also ask no questions. Both cleaning companies and the banks sacrifice security for the sake of a few bucks.

It's asking a lot of human nature to expect a man just out of prison to live on a starvation wage, with millions at his fingertips. Luckily, Fred turned honest! His story is typical—and it serves as a stark warning to the average depositor who thinks his neighborhood bank is as strong as the Rock of Gibraltar.

Brother, it ain't! And here's why . . .

Fred, with auto theft and armed robbery on his record, got a job with a small cleaning company through his Sing Sing parole board. The firm had cleaning contracts with banks, hotels, jewelry houses, etc.

After a few months as a cleaner in some of the New York hotels, Fred was asked by his boss if he'd like to switch to a bank. Naturally, the executive knew about Fred's record. The ex-convict was amazed, but said he'd like the job.

"I had visions of spending two weeks passing security tests and endless questioning," Fred told us. "All they asked me to do was to write my signature on two blank cards.

"Then they gave me the key to the front door of the bank."

The signature cards, Fred was told, were for the Protective Company's security test. As far as the ex-convict knows to this date, nothing was done to investigate him by the firm, a firm, one of many, which sells protective services.

The first day on the job a bank guard and a vice-president showed Fred, the ex-convict, how to turn off the electric alarm box. He was given a key to the door that unlocked the safety vault room in which depositors stored their valuables. He was asked no questions.

Fred went to work at three in the afternoon and remained there until midnight. For hours on end he was absolutely alone in the bank.

"If I'd wanted to play it crooked," Fred said, "all I had to do was to shut off the burglar alarm, go to the guards' lockers and take a couple of .38 revolvers and then start to work. I could have opened the safety deposit boxes with the proper tools in a few minutes' time.

"And if I wanted a cash haul I could have let in some other ex-cons with my key. All they had to do was to carry mops and pails for disguise. We then could have jimmied some of the vaults and escaped with a fortune. It's as easy as that."

That wasn't all Fred could have done.

Like similar institutions, this particular bank kept a collection of signature identification cards in small filing cabinets. These were unlocked—and the ex-convict had easy access to them. Had Fred been a forger he could easily have duplicated any of them. After all, the bank used these very records to verify signatures.

Fred worked at the bank a year, and when his employers lost their cleaning contract, he lost his job and took another one with a competitive outfit. They too asked him no questions and assigned him odd cleaning jobs, until finally, he again found himself with a pail and mop in another of the city's banks.

Here too, ex-convict Fred was told how to switch the burglar alarm off and on. He had access to a gun in the manager's desk. The vaults and the safety deposit boxes were within easy reach.

One of his jobs after the bank closed at 3:00 P.M. was to let in the representative of a check-cashing firm who made his deposits with a teller still on duty and left with his company's nightly supply of cash.

"It would have been a cinch to finger this guy for a stick-up," Fred said.

During his tenure at both banks, ex-con Fred had possession of the front-door keys at all times. He had endless opportunities to make duplicates—and a bank-door key commands a fancy price in the underworld.

Willie Sutton's sensational bank stick-ups are remembered not only because of the size of the hauls, but because of the outlaw's intimate knowledge of the banks he robbed. Ex-con cleaning men like Fred could have made blueprints of the institutions they worked at and sold them at a fat price to criminals like Sutton.

Fred stayed straight. But the cleaning companies who hire men like him, and the banks who accept this help without question, may not always be so lucky.

The bankers probably console themselves with the thought that employees of some cleaning companies are bonded. As a guarantee of an employee's character, however, that bond is worthless—and the cleaning companies know it—due to the practise of issuing "blanket bonds." This is done because the rapid turnover of help would make the cost of bonding each individual employee prohibitive.

In filling out the application for a bond, any ex-con is wise to the fact that to conceal his record, all he has to do is give as references the names of some cronies who live out of town. Even former cellmates are used for this purpose.

Many bonding companies don't have time for a painstaking check, nor can they afford the expense of minute checking.

Fred also worked for another cleaning firm that had many important contracts. "I used to hear on the prison grapevine while I was in Sing Sing," Fred said, "that this particular outfit was a good spot for any ex-con looking for a berth, since no questions were asked. Lots of their help had familiar faces and there were some guys with records a lot worse than mine."

True, many of these men, like Fred, probably are honest citizens today, their criminal careers behind them. But as long as there are unprincipled cleaning companies that will employ ex-convicts at starvation wages, asking no questions about their honesty, and as long as some financial institutions accept this fund of man-power with little regard for security—the depositor has a right to worry about his savings. And to ask the blunt question: "How safe is my bank?"

Playhouse Nightie . . .

CALL BOYS
OF MANHATTAN

This new twist to the world's oldest profession is happening right now! Women are the customers and virile college boys are the "Jezebels!"

ON THE EAST SIDE of Manhattan, all that glitters is probably gold—or guilt. Today, more merry Magdalenes live on or near Park Avenue than anywhere else in the world.

Theirs is the world's oldest profession . . . but trust the money-mad-anything-goes Gothamites to come up with a new twist, the world's newest profession standing side-by-side with the oldest.

It's a dignified four-story town house in New York's fashionable East Sixties. At least, that's how the neighbors see it.

But that's not the way it really is. This house, modest and unimposing, is one of the hottest layouts in Manhattan. It's a playground for babes—a place where women with an urge to merge are entertained by college boys.

It's also the spiciest operation New York has harbored since 1940, when the License Commissioner booted out a Male Escort Service which offered escorts to lonesome ladies at so much per evening. The Escort Service ended when authorities feared that it might eventually turn into an erotic enterprise.

In this new operation the sky is the limit, but it's safer—and a lot quieter!

The inmates are college boys. They come from New York, and from various other campuses all over the country. They're working their way through college and they love their work. Dames are paying for their diplomas.

The "madame" of the house is a middle-aged nance. Put this "madame" in a Homburg and he'd look like one of our diplomats carrying dispatches of destiny. Except that his destiny is sex-hungry females who just want to have fun, friendship, or what have you.

Digging up customers is no problem for this devious deviate. Word of his boudoir bazaar is the hush-hush tidbit in swank night-life powder rooms and plush cocktail lounges all over Gotham.

The clients fall into three categories: (1)—Married women who want to do a little safe cheating; (2)—Career girls who want to have their fun quietly and forget it quickly; (3) —Society playgirls with time on their hands and money to burn.

Once past the brass knocker on the old oaken door, there's a bucketful of bawdiness. Inside, a babe pays her money and takes her choice. There's a variety of types, all of them genuine college boys. They all cost the same—50 dollars for an hour, more or less, of intimate companionship. The kind you don't read about in text books.

It's the most bizarre cash-and-tarry business sin has set up in a long time, and operates strictly by appointment through a telephone answering service. The sly gimmick keeps this operation from being wire-tapped by the law.

Here, in surroundings reminiscent of the lush bordello operated by former madame Polly Adler, females in pursuit of passion can pick, pay and play with any Joe College type that appeals to them. And there's no rush. They can sit and swap charm for cash in an elegant private nook, or sip a Martini in a corner of the intimate little cocktail lounge that was once a drawing room. They can even order hors d'oeuvres from the kitchen. And when the preliminaries are over, they can repair to one of the old brownstone's cozy boudoirs.

The "steadies" are the local collegians. The out-of-towners work summer vacations and school holidays. Their cut is 40% of the total fee. Plus tips, which are heavy. Average take for the boys is $300 per week each, which isn't too much, considering.

The "madame" digs up his male commodities by posing as an old grad of whatever campus he happens to be soliciting. He's got more old school ties than the halls of learning have ivy. And it's a cinch he's not as green.

Like any smart businessman, he knows it takes time to train

these students fresh from the campus. After all, even a 40% take isn't high when energy is expended too freely.

Conservation is the watchword.

But after the first week, a novice quickly learns his job. We heard about one young sophomore who was asked by a female customer if he weren't afraid of being arrested for practicing prostitution.

"Not me, ma'am," the collegian drawled. "I ain't practisin' no more. I know how now."

We had a tough time getting a former lover boy to spill this story. It shocked us just as much as it is probably shocking you. But it's all here and going full blast. Incidentally, this particular lad was one of the most popular in the place. No wonder, he had dispensed his charms before. He was being maintained by a small town lady of means when he was picked up on a Midwestern campus.

He didn't mind joining the male stable. While he needed the money, he also happened to love the work. So do most of the others. Remember, it's one of those places where everybody kisses but nobody tells.

Among other things we discovered is that the male magdalene charmers last about two months. At least, the city boys do. They say the wear and tear is terrific . . . but worth it. The out-of-town collegians usually take over during the summer months. Some of them also return the following year. For post-graduate work, no doubt.

If you're wondering what becomes of these scarlet males, we can tell you that most of them drift back to the conventional way of life. Some tie up with former clients, sub rosa or legally, and occasionally one pops up who has gone on to bigger and better things. There is one alumnus of this sin salon whom you now see frequently on television dramatic shows.

At any rate, chic Park Avenue has its Babylon for babes where the lambs pursue the wolves, but how long it will last is still the big question.

Want the phone number? You won't find it in the yellow pages, but it's not that hard to get your hands on it. A subtle sawbuck to a hip headwaiter should produce the magic number. If that fails, just ask around. Who knows—even your best friends might tell you.

And remember: if a man answers, don't hang up!

Hotel Hustlers . . .

HOW HOTELS GET
TAKEN FOR A BUNDLE

Even the best hotels are suckers for clever swindles. Here are a couple of new ones that have some of the city's smartest house dicks hopping.

WHEN YOU AND your wife check into your favorite hotel you expect the usual top-flight service. If you don't get it you put up a loud squawk, as you have every right to do. And that can put the hotel on a spot. If you're a regular and valued guest, they might have to give you *too much* service, and get hooked by a slick racket in the process.

For instance: anxious to keep you happy, a desk clerk will cheerfully accept packages for you, sometimes even anteing up C.O.D. charges which are later added to your bill. That's where the con man comes in, and that's where a package can cost the hotel a bundle.

Here's how it operates:

You are Mr. Jones, and your hotel loves you to pieces. You spend plenty, tip well and don't annoy the other guests. So the management figures that if a C.O.D. package arrives for you it's smart business to shell out the money and, "We'll take it up with Mr. Jones later."

Unfortunately, nobody knows that better than the swindler, and here's how he sets the stage for a fast buck.

The hotel desk receives a phone call. A man's voice says he is Mr. Jones of Room 405. That's you, remember? But it's *not* you calling; you're busy at the office. The caller explains that he had been to his jeweler to have an old family heirloom stone reset in a new ring. It's to be delivered this afternoon and it's to be a surprise for his wife, "So please don't mention anything to her about it." And by all means, *don't* send the package up to the room.

Would the desk kindly oblige Mr. Jones by paying the C.O.D. charges and holding the package until he picks it up? The cost will be about $95."

The desk clerk who takes the call says the management will be delighted, particularly since "Mr. Jones" has been so kind as to notify them in advance, thus relieving them of a possible wrong decision.

The swindle has started to function smoothly. How did the crook get your name and room number? How does he know your hours? Who knows? Possibly a confederate working in the hotel tipped him off. Anyway, he also knows that the hotel's work shift changes over at 4 P.M., and that time is important to his plan. With one shift of clerks turning over duties and instructions to another, there is a certain amount of confusion, and confusion helps in a fast con game.

Promptly at 4 P.M. a clean-cut young man arrives at the hotel, goes up to the desk, and states his errand. He is delivering the package of jewelry, C.O.D., as requested by Mr. Jones. The charges are $94.75. A harried clerk finds a note okaying the transaction, accepts the small parcel and turns over the money. Right here the gyp has an ace in the hole.

If any question is raised, he says he'll gladly take the stuff back and get in touch with Mr. Jones later. And he is extra careful to keep the amount under $100, so if he *is* nabbed, the rap is only a misdemeanor.

So, he pockets the $94.75 and fades.

You, Mr. Jones of Room 405, arrive at 6 P.M., as usual, and as usual, stop at the desk for mail or messages. The clerk on duty hands you the small package without comment. After all, it's been paid for. You are puzzled because you haven't ordered anything, but you figure the little woman must have bought some trinket or other, so you slip the thing in your pocket and head for your room.

You kiss Mrs. Jones and hand her the package, muttering it must be for her. Mrs. J. is puzzled too, but being a woman, she's also curious, so she opens it. Well, there's a ring there all right, but it's certainly no heirloom—it's the kind you might buy for laughs at the five-and-dime! There follows a call to the hotel desk, with a shocked—and expensive—gasp at the other end of the line.

You haven't ordered any merchandise, either C.O.D. or otherwise. And you *certainly* have not authorized any payment of cash to anybody.

The receiver clicks. The hotel has been taken—to the tune of $94.75—with as neat a swindle as was ever pulled. You, of course, are not responsible. The clean-cut young man? He's long gone with his loot. All the management can do is circulate his description and hope he'll be collared the next time he tries that little racket.

The house sadly crosses out that $94.75 item they've already entered on your bill, and charges off the loss to bitter experience. They've been had—but good.

Moral: if your favorite hotel should ever refuse to accept C.O.D. deliveries unless you get up the cash, don't blow your top . . . Now you know the reason why.

LIVING IT UP ON THE CUFF

THE DELIVERY PACKAGE routine is only petty larceny compared to this swindle the four-flushers have dreamed up for a free ride in the city's ritziest hostelries. The fraud has been driving hardened hotel dicks to tears and wilting the carnation on many a manager's otherwise impeccable lapel.

One sunny day last Fall, a well-dressed man stepped out of a cab in front of one of Manhattan's swank hotels. A brace of bellboys rushed forward to help him and escorted him to the registration desk. There he signed in, giving as his home address a distant Western city. Mr. A asked for and was given a luxurious suite, one of the hotel's finest and most expensive accommodations. Cost—$40 a day.

He picked up his key, dispatched his luggage to his rooms, tipped the bellboys generously, and walked out of the hotel to meet a confederate at a nearby restaurant. A half-hour later, the confederate, Mr. B, turns up at the hotel, lugging his own suitcases to the registration desk. There he asks for and receives one of the smallest—and least expensive—rooms in the house. Cost—$8 a day.

Within minutes after being shown to his room, Swindler B goes to A's suite, knocks quietly, and is allowed in. Then the boys really go to work. The man with the cheap room moves some clothing to A's luxurious set-up, but leaves enough stuff in his own place to make it seem that he still lives there. And every night he goes back to the little room to rumple the bed as if he'd slept in it.

For the next week, life is one long party for the two swindlers. They enjoy the best of everything the hotel has to offer in the $40 per day suite, from epicurean steak dinners to fawning valet service. There's always plenty of booze and broads. They even charge expensive shirts, suits and topcoats from the shops in the hotel, which are only too glad to serve a guest.

Then, on the seventh day, swindler A finds an envelope in his box. Upstairs he shows the itemized bill to B. It comes to $1800, including the hotel's five per cent tax.

Not to be topped, B pulls out his own envelope. "Here's our real bill. Fifty-six dollars plus tax. Let's get ready to blow this joint."

The two move swiftly and efficiently. Swindler A packs his clothes and Mr. B furtively shifts A's baggage to his own room. Then Mr. A, as jaunty as Casanova after a conquest, strolls out of the hotel and is never seen again.

Mr. B, in his turn, calls for a bellboy to take his bags downstairs, pays his $56 bill, and smiles at the desk clerk as he leaves.

He has good reason to smile. He and his partner have lived a week of luxury in the greatest city in the world, practically on the cuff. They've dined and wined magnificently, drew cash for immediate expenses, got their theatre tickets on credit, and even walked off with new wardrobes charged to the hotel shops.

Unbelievable? Not at all. Wasn't Mr. A considered an affluent guest with a luxurious suite?

And the hotel? Well, they've collected $56, plus tax, a rumpled bed, and an uncollectable tab for $1800.

Next time you think a hotel manager's life is easy, just remember that the accomplished swindler can make it tough on anyone.

Misery Mile . . .

BLOOD FOR BOOZE

It's flirting with death to give your blood more than once in six weeks . . . But on the Bowery it's worth at least five bucks a pint, so the hooch-hungry bums go back again and again to a line that can lead straight to the morgue!

TWO DOZEN RUN-DOWN firetraps that call themselves hotels, where fifteen cents buys a flop on a bare wood floor. Five dozen "horse markets"—the world's cheapest restaurants where the hamburger ran last at Hialeah. And a countless number of bars where the Sweet Lucy is ten cents a glass and the atmosphere is thrown in for free.

The shuffling men in threadbare overcoats and cardboard shoes have a name for the place. They call it Misery Mile, because it's a full mile of human distress running from Cooper Square to Chatham Square.

It's the Bowery.

And the rheumy-eyed, broken-down, empty-eyed men who live and drink and die there live only for their daily ration of alcohol. They'll do anything in the world for a drink.

They'll even sell the blood right out of their veins!

That's right—they exchange their blood for booze. And if within the past year or two, you or a member of your family had to receive a transfusion in a hospital, could be that the whole blood or plasma came from a member of this army of derelicts.

What does this mean to you? Well, it could mean death! There are any number of viruses—science has yet to discover *how* many—which simply can not be detected by microscopic or other examination. Jaundice, for example, is one of the big dangers which can't be discovered by even the most meticulous tests. And jaundiced blood administered to a gravely ill patient in a hospital might very well be fatal. It happened many times on the battlefields during World War II and less often but still far too many times in civilian life since then.

If this practice claims only a limited number in the hospitals, it widens its arms to engulf a multitude of pathetic, broken-down "donors" every year by bleeding them to death. For blood is big business.

But let's watch one of the bums peddle his life away. He's just slept off many rounds of rotgut in a hallway, a park bench or, if he had four-bits, on a cot in a flop house. He stumbles to the nearest blood bank and as he shuffles along, the derelict's one alcohol-logged thought is to get that fast buck. Five of them, in fact. Five dollars for a pint of blood. That will buy a lot of cheap whiskey in Manhattan's Bowery.

In some cities, other than New York, some blood banks carry the grim business even farther with lures in the want ad sections of the papers headlined: "NEED $4? DO THIS NOW!"

The come-on then promises "Earn $4 and up, right now, for regular donations and up to $75, if you have the right type."

It's one of the cruelest hoaxes on record. Few of the sodden "winos" in those cities, who grab for this bait ever have that elusive seventy-five buck brand of blood. They pour their lives out of their arms at the minimum four bucks a crack.

The average panhandler in New York usually has a list of the City's blood banks in his pocket. He checks it. Last week he went to one blood bank. Day before yesterday he went to another. He can't hit the same ones too fast; he's got to make the rounds.

He's staggering, because he may give two pints a week and you don't keep in the pink of condition on a diet of rotgut while you are selling the most precious thing in your body—your blood.

So he goes to one of the city's blood banks on his list. He is given a thorough examination—temperature, pulse, blood pressure. He's questioned at length about his medical history. The blood bank tries to check him in every detail. They will reject him if he is giving his blood too often, or if he admits that he has had jaundice or malaria. But the bum has been through this a dozen times and he knows the right answers. And who can tell when a Bowery derelict is telling the truth?

So he goes to the bleeding room. A pint is drained from his arm. A serology (chemical analysis of the blood) is taken. No trace of communicable diseases shows up. And he gets his five bucks and away he goes, pallid under his grime, his walk slow and wobbly, headed for the nearest Bowery gin mill.

He's also headed for the morgue!

These Bowery outcasts are killing themselves quickly with this device to raise dough for their insatiable thirst.

Health and police officials are noting the upward swing of "death by natural causes" among the bums. And often the arm of the corpse shows the scars of repeated punctures.

He bled to death to get his booze.

All of the city's blood banks are licensed by the Health Department and their standards are rigid. They check donors carefully and refuse to draw blood more frequently than once every eight weeks; and seldom more than five times a year from one donor. Yet, because of a desperate need for the buck, many derelicts manage somehow to sell their blood as often as twenty times a year.

The commercial blood bank pays five dollars a pint, sells it to hospitals at from ten dollars to twenty dollars per pint. And on your hospital bill, it's thirty-five dollars or even more, unless friends or relatives agree to replace it by giving blood at the rate of two pints for every pint you have received in the hospital.

The Red Cross, of course, does not pay. The blood is donated and in turn supplied without cost. But during peace time, the average person is not too anxious to give up his time, energy and blood. A local disaster, followed by radio and newspaper appeals, usually brings prompt response from patriotic citizens. But in the demanding day-to-day work of medical science, whole blood is often scarce.

As a result some derelicts would show up the day following a bleeding and try to sell another pint. The smart down-and-outers follow a pattern. In big cities like New York they hit a different blood bank once a week or more, if they can get away with it. Then they move on from one city to another.

The blood banks are supposed to be taking blood to save lives. Instead, men are being bled to death, and, ironically, the blood banks can't seem to do too much about it, although every effort is being made by them to curb this wave of self-destruction for bucks to buy booze.

In addition to alcoholics, law enforcement agencies and blood banks are worried about the increasing number of drug addicts who seek out blood banks to obtain money to satisfy their craving.

The Red Cross, the Blood Transfusion Association and all licensed public and commercial blood banks will, of course, have nothing to do with these junkies. The tell-tale needle punctures give them away and even though such addiction is not communicable through the blood, reputable organizations will not touch such a person.

You can recognize the licensed blood bank by the type of examination given the prospective blood donor. If you have had malaria or jaundice, you are rejected. Ditto for victims of diabetes, TB or any active heart ailment. Also, blood will be rejected from ulcer victims or those with rheumatic fever. Your weight is checked. You must present proper identification and a careful record is kept of your description, your condition and time of last visit.

The commercial blood banks pay the standard five dollars but you must wait until the serology is completed. If diseases show up in the test, you are not paid and a note is made to reject you if you show up again.

Yet, in spite of all this, the tragic irony continues—the blood that is bought to save lives can be the blood that is draining out a life for that five dollars and a round of drinks.

A Dream Scheme . . .

UNCLE SAM IS HANDLING HORSE BETS BY MAIL!

Because of a strange court decision, the smiling man in gray who delivers your mail has been turned into an errand boy for a ring of bookmakers!

THE UNITED STATES Post Office Department—always eager to lower the boom on improper use of the mails—is about to play stooge to one of the biggest mail-order gambling operations of all time.

As you read this, a couple of smart New York bookies are

calmly getting ready to use Uncle Sam's 127,000 mail carriers as "runners" for a multi-million dollar horse book via a Nevada pipeline.

That's right, we're talking about the same stern, righteous old Post Office Department that cracks down on sweepstakes tickets, says "No, no!" to lotteries, and even gets stuffy over such relatively insignificant gimmicks as chain letters.

Now this prim, law-conscious arm of the Federal Government is unknowingly going to soil its official hands by taking and delivering bets—thousands of them—on horses, and most of them sucker bets, at that. The cost? It will come out of the taxpayer's pocket, because the government already loses money on a four-cent stamp.

Not that the Postmaster General or his minions are going to stand on street corners or in front of cigar stores jotting down side-of-the-mouth wagers on the third at Jamaica. But it will add up to the same thing when the hayburner book gets under way at Las Vegas and postmen all over the country start picking up mail-order bets, and delivering winnings—if any—to the players.

In planning their deal, the New York sharpies are simply adapting an already successful mail-order horse betting operation for their own purposes. What they're doing actually, is lifting a page from the Caliente Future Book. For years, the operators of this book, with headquarters in Tijuana, Mexico, have been harvesting a huge crop of U.S. dollars with the cooperation of the United States Post Office and its mail carriers. They have been booking bets from American horse players, through the U.S. mails and, believe it or not, the Post Office cannot refuse to carry them because of an incredible court decision that makes everything nice and legal.

The Broadway bookmakers reasoned that if the dream

scheme pulled in pesos south of the border, why couldn't it pay off even bigger up north—with the same cooperation from the Post Office, of course?

Furthermore, the average horse player would much rather mail his bets to a bookie in the United States than all the way to Mexico. Patriotism has nothing to do with it; it's just safer.

So here's how the New York gambling combine is going to work it. They are already busy compiling a list of thousands upon thousands of inveterate horse players. Months before an important stake race, like the Kentucky Derby, the Preakness, or the Santa Anita Handicap, the branch office in Vegas will start handling mail sack after mail sack of folders going out to horse bettors throughout the nation.

These folders will list the names of one hundred or more horses nominated for any given race, with accompanying odds. Seldom will more than fifteen or twenty actually go to the post, but some of the odds quoted will be sky-high enough to make a bangtail backer drool all over his scratch sheet. For example, let's say he scans the roster and picks a nag quoted at 1,000-to-1. All he has to do is to fill out a coupon, enclose his check or money order, and drop his dream bet in the near-est mail box.

Uncle Sam then steps back into the picture and dispatches his sore-bunion boys to relay the wager to Las Vegas, the drop for the New York bookies.

If by some miracle this long shot should not only run but also stumble home in front, the pay-off will be on the basis of the early 1,000-to-1 odds, as attested by the postmarked envelope. And again the postal service will be ready to help out, this time by delivering the jackpot to the winner's door—without getting a cut of the profits.

But as any hep horse player knows, a future book makes no

refunds on scratches (a "scratched" horse is one which is withdrawn from the field of starters), and the chances are that the enticing 1,000-to-1 shot—along with a whole herd of other nondescript horseflesh—will never go to the post.

Which means, of course, that the United States Post Office Department will have helped the bookies stash away a real bundle of boob money by saddle-up time.

The whole operation appears strictly legit, too. Since about every form of gambling is okay in Nevada, all the mail-order bookie has to do is to take out a federal gambling tax stamp—and he's in business, which is why the New York mob is smart enough to operate through the Vegas pipeline.

As for betting through the mails, a lower-court federal judge in Illinois ruled eleven years ago (United States vs. Rich, et al, April 3, 1950) that such activity did not constitute a "lottery, gift, enterprise, or similar scheme" as prohibited by statute.

And so there you have it—the United States Post Office is in active, if unwilling, partnership in a horse book. The New York-Vegas operation—like its Mexican counterpart—should turn out to be a very successful deal, too. After all, as long as there are long shots, there will always be suckers to play them.

Especially when Uncle Sam makes it all so handy by handling the bets.

**She's not a Call Girl —
She's not a Party Girl —
She is...**

THE SEX-A-PHONE GIRL

She's a real smart chick with a new routine. Her ad reads: "Want to see more of me? Call me day or night. My phone number is . . . . . . "

FROM THE TIME Peter Stuyvesant cast a leering Dutch eye over the chubby damsels who made life more pleasant for Manhattan's earliest white settlers, sex has been a big business in the Big Town. In those days, sex appeal and sex were synonymous. A girl was either completely virtuous or she put a price on her physical properties.

As the years rolled by, prostitution came to occupy a specific place in the community. The Tenderloin district, located on what is now the site of New York's teeming garment center, was the town's most famous red-light district. And everyone from high-brows to hijackers took advantage of the largest beef trust east of Chicago.

During the "Roaring Twenties," the mobsters moved in and made vice a corporate concern, opening a string of whorehouses from Greenwich Village to Harlem, from which profits were demanded and dividends declared.

Later, when vice investigations and reform movements slowed traffic in the red-light areas, sex became subtler and in many ways more interesting. The pimp and the prostitute became the exception rather than the rule. Sure, the streetwalker still sold her wares, but she'd lost status. So the girls began to use their sex appeal—without giving away or selling their bodies.

The strip-tease artist became the new national sex symbol —and the panting patrons flocked to the burlesque houses to see the girls take it off right down to the last G-string.

Then came the dance hall hostess and the taxi dancer, who could be virtuous if they wanted to be, giving the slobbering sap a swift shake and a feel for his money, but no more.

The B-girl, hired by the saloon keepers, was an interesting example of cashing in on sex without actually selling it. She usually lured the bar patron into spending a wad on watered hooch. Then she intimated that she'd be glad to go home with him. The glassy-eyed patron would nod, then be helped to a waiting taxi where the chump and the chippie would take a long ride home. He'd usually pass out before the ride ended and would be dumped on a lonely road—minus his wallet.

Later sex became even more vicarious as the in-the-flesh girls faded out on to the printed page and undressed photos of the photographer's model became the rage. Commercial sex appeal consisted of bare babes displayed on the pages of hundreds of cheap pin-up magazines—sold over the counter and under the counter at a quarter a copy. These were the thrill seekers' delight, who were willing to look without touching at these bargain prices.

This doesn't mean that the scarlet sister, the practitioner of the oldest profession in the world, just faded out and disappeared. She was all there, all right, but she just wasn't elegant unless she happened to work in one of the rare sporting houses from which only the most respectable, virtuous and civic-minded politicians took their cut.

But you can't keep a good idea down, and the chippies and the cheats latched on to a twentieth-century device with a bang. Alexander Graham Bell's little black telephone was put to use by the merry Magdalenes in a novel and fascinating way and thus was born the call girl.

By the 1950s, the call girl was as much a part of the Manhattan scene as the skyline. She was chic, smart and in demand. She definitely had class and she charged for it. The out-of-town buyers, the local playboys, the well-heeled executives and the sporting set were happy to date the call girl . . . and to be seen with her. This was something new. What she did with the boys in the wee hours was her own business . . . and business was good.

Then the bubble burst. An heir to an oleomargarine fortune was caught pimping for a stable-full of fillies of the night.

The cops clamped down, and the call girl found it more difficult to operate.

But as the defense grows tighter, the offense gets smarter . . . and so has evolved the highest form of sex salesmanship yet devised. It took a smart, slick chick to think it up and she's been cleaning up faster than a crapshooter on his hottest days. And what's more, her sex-selling racket is perfectly legal.

Here's how it works. In thousands of telephone booths around Manhattan our sharp little doll has plastered miniature stickers with her sexy kisser, come-on smile and the provocative invitation: "Want to see more of me? Call me day or night." And her phone number is right under the picture.

This naturally would catch any gent's eye, so guys by the thousands have dialed this delectable doll's number. In fact, we dialed it ourselves and after hours of getting a busy signal, finally heard her soft, sultry voice. Her purring pitch went like this:

"Hello darling. I'm glad you called. I've been waiting to hear from you. Would love to make your acquaintance with four lovely, tempting pictures of myself. Please write to Box . . . and enclose two dollars for which I will promptly mail you the photos."

Her pitch, of course, is a recording, but that doesn't matter. You hear the promise in her voice and practically feel her lips on your ear, and so the wolves can't wait to fork across the two dollars she asks for the photos.

Before jumping to erroneous conclusions and phoning the Post Office's pornography squad, you'd better take a deep breath and relax. Our little sharpie does exactly what she's promised the suckers. You see more of her alright, plenty more, but in a way that would satisfy good old Aunt Mathilda.

She sends four pictures of herself, all full-length. Only she's clothed from stem to stern and all the way up to the collarbone. No postal inspector could ask for anything more . . . unless he happened to be one of the telephone wolves.

Which is very possible because in New York, anything can happen—if there's a telephone handy.

95

Crooks in White Collars . . .

SWINDLERS ON
YOUR DOORSTEP

Fast-talking con men, posing as G-men are hooking gullible housewives with a new, penny-ante racket!

THE UNSUSPECTING AMERICAN housewife has long been the prey for every conceivable type of hustler and pitchman who knocks on her door, but there's a new type of chiseler roaming the big town who threatens to become a real menace.

Don't be fooled by his insidious racket.

So that you'll recognize this newest breed of pilfering para-site, here is the way he operates. An officious-looking guy knocks on the door of a house or an apartment and claims to be an FBI agent. To make it look legit, he flashes a leather folder with his photograph and phony credentials.

Then he'll ask you where you have been making your pur-chases in the neighborhood. When you tell him, he will say that these are the very places where counterfeit money has been passed and that in making change, these stores have un-wittingly flooded the neighborhood with counterfeit. He is sorry to inconvenience you, he'll say, but the FBI is trying to check up on all this bogus dough.

Now comes his gimmick. He will then ask you to show him all the cash you have around the house and when you do, he will pronounce most, if not all of it, counterfeit and ask you to accompany him to the police station for identification pur-poses.

While you nervously disappear to put on a dab of lipstick or to get your coat, this phony will quickly fade out of your apartment and you will never see him or your money again.

You might be telling yourself, "I'm not that stupid. No-body could ever pull that one on me." But this slick dodge has been worked successfully around New York, and women have not been the only suckers. Many an innocent guy, quak-ing in his boots, has dutifully handed over his dough after the impersonating agent flashes his phony FBI identification.

One fast-talking hustler pulled this swindle on more than eighty-two persons in a single Manhattan neighborhood, be-fore he was nailed, and there's no telling how many other con men are getting away with it at this very moment.

The psychological element is this thief's strongest weapon. The mere fact that an FBI agent calls on a citizen seems to be enough to fluster the intended victims and put them on the defensive. They know they are innocent, but they just dread getting mixed up in this sort of intrigue. They become so anxious to co-operate that they are soon putty in the swindler's hands and will believe almost anything he tells them.

Naturally, every law-abiding citizen wants to co-operate with the FBI, but remember, the law is on your side and if you have the slightest suspicions, assert them. That's one way to nip this racket in the bud.

Another thing to remember is that FBI agents usually travel in pairs, so be wary of a lone agent who seeks you out.

If anyone purporting to be a law enforcement officer knocks on your door and asks to see your money, tell him you'll be with him as soon as you make a phone call to check with your police station or local FBI office. If he's a legitimate agent, he will welcome this corroboration.

If he's a phony, you can be sure he will be gone by the time you lift up your phone receiver—and you will not only have saved yourself some money, but you'll have helped to put a crimp in this nasty racket.

Not-so-tender tenderfeet . . .

SNAP, CRACKLE AND POP PARTIES

Juvenile delinquents have discovered a new kick—"ammies"—to "send" them on a three-minute trip to the moon!

P ACKED IN A yellow box, a dozen ampules to the carton, they look like pieces of hard candy, individually wrapped in bright orange mesh.

But no box of candy ever carried the warning stamped on these little packages. In fire-engine red, and repeated twice for additional emphasis, is the warning—POISON.

Even that doesn't faze the anything-for-a-thrill kids. They've adopted the dangerous drug amyl nitrite, nicknamed the ampules "ammies," and are using them for jet-propelled three-minute kicks impudently titled "trips to the moon," or "snap, crackle and pop parties."

The drug has a legitimate use, of course. Victims of certain heart ailments carry amyl nitrite at all times. When struck by an attack, they snap open one of the tiny glass ampules and get sudden, explosive relief by sniffing the pungent fumes.

The flip name for these teen-age shindigs is actually a telegraphic report of what happens to an ammie sniffer. He snaps the glass vial, crackles it in his hand as he sniffs the stuff, then pops right off this earth. His face turns brick red and he feels as though he were floating on a cloud. The effect lasts about three minutes, after which it wears off, leaving a horrible odor in the nostrils and often a violent headache.

The junior jive gangs buy a few quarts of beer and a box of ammies—a dozen sell for about two dollars—and they're set for an evening of supersonic sailing. The beer slightly prolongs the effect of sniffing and serves to deaden the subsequent violent headache.

Having ammies in one's possession is not illegal, but selling them without a prescription is.

Nevertheless, bootleg amyl nitrite is being peddled openly, and in Little Puerto Rico—that teeming, swarming section of New York, around East 102nd Street, a focal point for juvenile delinquents—purchase of the stuff can be made without difficulty.

One reason the snap, crackle and pop craze has spread like wildfire is that thrill-kid users have introduced new recruits to the dangerous fad by insisting ammies are harmless. This fiction often tempts cautious kids who have successfully resisted temptations to have a fling at narcotics.

A noted child guidance director, speaking for a group of his colleagues, warned that it is time a nation-wide crackdown was ordered on ammies. "We have learned to our regret that amyl nitrite almost invariably leads to more deadly habits," he said. "To kids, those snap, crackle and pop parties may be fun; to us they're just what it says on the box—POISON."

Slander for Sale . . .

THE WHISPER MERCHANTS

If you hear a malicious rumor on your bus or subway, don't spread it . . . it's a cinch a rumor factory has been well paid to plant that whisper in your ear.

EﮯﮯﮯVER HEAR OF A rumor factory? Well, don't look now but the guy who is whispering in your ear could be working for one.

Did your cabbie ever tell you that it's a shame a certain large restaurant chain is allowed to operate in a city like New York because it is anti-Semitic and refuses to hire Jews? Has your elevator operator ever whispered that he just heard a certain tobacco firm mixes some ersatz compound with the tobacco in its cigarettes to save money . . . and that you're a sure bet to get lung cancer if you keep smoking them?

This insidious slander is not just mere gossip. It's *paid whispering*, launched by a New York slander outfit whose specific racket is starting whisper campaigns. If a business man wants to smash a rival firm, or a politician wants to wreck an opponent's chances, he can hire professional whisperers on any scale the freight will allow. This Manhattan slander foundry will rent out whisperers at $25 a day and up, and they are equipped to operate everywhere.

Scurrilous whispers can be tremendously potent weapons— so powerful that you and you and you have sometime or another been an unwitting employee of one of these "knife-in-the-back" outfits. That's part of the set-up and here's how it operates:

For purposes of illustration let's take a candy firm that is out to put a crimp in the business of a competitor. The rumor factory will supply the unscrupulous client with two whisperers. They usually work in groups, but one pair would be enough in this instance.

The whisperers would board busses in the early morning rush and in a stentorian tone that is supposed to be a confidential whisper, one would say to the other, "Guess that finishes off the X Candy Company. Friend of mine over at the Board of Health told me—off the record, of course—that it was reported that roaches were found in X Company's candy. Seems it happened a couple of times before but they paid off the people and killed the story."

By now all ears within hearing range in the bus have perked

103

up and, whether the passengers in the bus believe the story or not, a goodly number of them will repeat it when they get to their offices or their homes. Not only will they repeat it, but human nature being what it is, they will elaborate on the story.

The whisperers will spend the full day in as many public places as possible, such as elevators, bars, and other spots where gossip is most likely to be picked up. Some of the best bets for their vilifying rumors are cab drivers, barbers and beauty shops. From there on, the insidious whisper snowballs.

Under these circumstances, a whisper is really not a whisper, but a thunderclap that can reverberate from coast to coast with the fleet contagion of the plague.

Two pairs of lips can give frightening impetus to one well-planted whisper, as many business men, politicians and personalities who have been victims of such whispering campaigns have discovered.

Probably the most maligned victim of the commercial scandal factory over the past few decades was the late Franklin D. Roosevelt. The hate groups systematically spread all sorts of fantastic stories about F.D.R. You yourself have undoubtedly heard the most common gossip about him—the one that insisted the name Roosevelt was a streamlined version of his "real" name—Rosenfeld. It was completely false and baseless, of course, and it all started with a paid whisper.

When Adlai Stevenson was a candidate for the presidency, he, too, was a victim of a vicious whispering campaign, although the stories had no foundation whatsoever.

And the latest and best known victim of the whisper merchants was President John F. Kennedy. Many were the false and scurrilous rumors that were spread about him, utterly without foundation, when he ran for office. Make no mistake about this . . . those were whispers for pay!

A prominent white TV singing star once found herself powerless to combat the vicious insinuations that she had Negro blood and had crossed the line to pass as a white woman —another victim of the propaganda merchants.

Many industries have suffered immeasurable loss through the slander of the paid defamers. A home permanent wave kit was almost forced off the market after professional whisperers circulated the rumor that the product had burned the scalps of many women all over the country, causing them to become bald overnight.

Restaurants also have been among the most vulnerable victims of these paid muckrakers. A few well-dropped whispers about an unsanitary kitchen, and whether the regular customer believes the story or not, he begins to feel a little squeamish about going into the place.

Some malicious gossip about Chinese restaurants was once circulated by competitors. The buzz was that some of the kitchen staff was discovered to be suffering from hepatitis. The story was untrue, of course, but for a time it got so that many people associated all Chinese restaurants with the dread malady.

Some of the lushest pickings for the whisper merchants have been in Wall Street, where more than one ill-founded rumor has cost men fortunes. The whisper is spread in the form of a tip that a certain stock is due for a big rise. This type of information is usually balm for the sucker's ear. He will start buying—and often the buying wave will send the stock soaring. But after the boys have made their killing, the stock will fall so low it won't be worth using for wall paper.

Fight managers and football coaches have used the paid whisper to spread rumors about their teams or their gladiators. Usually the whisper is the exact opposite of the fact. If they're in good shape, the story is spread that they've been secretly ill and don't stand a chance.

Another devastating form of the whispering campaign is the personal vendetta, where an individual will hire this lip service to injure some personal enemy by spreading a scurrilous story about the victim. This is closely akin to the old witch-burning days when a woman would be burned at the stake after her enemies spread the word that she was a witch.

So listen all you want in the subway, on your bus or even to your cabbie, but if you must repeat, remember that you might be doing—for free—the dirty work of the whisper merchants. They get paid for it.

Naughty! Naughty!

PARLOR, BEDROOM AND BABE . . .

Typewriter tootsies are working the plush hotels. And they know just what to do for tired business men who end a letter with a proposition instead of a preposition!

F OR THE FLUSH tourist and expense-account traveller alike, Manhattan's chrome-and-steel hotels offer every service imaginable. Efficient employees will walk your dog, shine your shoes, press your pants, amuse your children, run errands, mail your letters, cash your checks, and nine times out of ten, wind up with your money.

And, believe it or not, breakfast isn't all you can have in bed!

We're not talking about the play-for-pay cuties who have an in with the bell captain. The professional prossies working hotels are an old story—as a matter of fact, they're hard to find in the good New York hotels. The management spends big money keeping them out. However, throwing a ten spot to a bellhop will still bring a bundle of curves to your door if you're holed up in a dive, but that's not the way it works in many first-class hotels.

Now the dolls who know how to tickle a typewriter have a brand-new slant, and it's a dilly. See for yourself . . .

Neat gold lettering on the swank hotel's office door says *"Secretarial Service"* and inside the room typewriters clatter and telephones buzz.

Now and again one of the pretty young things seated at small desks answers the phone, applies fresh lipstick to her mouth, snaps shut an expensive portable typewriter, then trips smartly to a bank of elevators in the huge hotel and soars upstairs to take a letter from a visiting executive.

Tell a playboy, not in the know, that this crisply efficient scene is being used by some naughty stenos to peddle a side line of sex—and he'd laugh in your face. But that's just what's been going on in a number of Manhattan hotels. Some of the town's sassier typewriter tootsies have worked out a slick, fool-proof scheme to add substantially to their income. They simply throw in an extra added attraction to their stenographic services . . . love for sale!

As employees of the hotel secretarial service, the type-and-tarry cuties have a made-to-order clientele for their extra-curricular activities amongst the visiting businessmen who want to dictate a letter. A red light on the hotel switchboard has dispossessed the red light over the door.

The owners of the hotel secretarial service concessions are completely unaware of this set-up and, in addition, most hotels maintain top security officers to crack down on just such shenanigans. But the racket continues to flourish.

The angle is as safe as government bonds and a lot simpler. It hides behind an innocent phrase they scribble on the office work sheets, when they return from two and three-hour calls to wealthy guests of the hotel, with no letters to type and not a word of dictation in their shorthand books.

They simply log their names, the amount of time spent on the job and in the space where a description of their work is required, the words—"Secretarial Services."

Those words cover the scarlet stenos every bit as nicely as the blankets they often find themselves under. So far as the hotel and the public stenographers' office are concerned, "Secretarial Services" means a host of perfectly legitimate tasks; answering the telephone for a harried out-of-town businessman in conference with important buyers, or going shopping for him.

Many a legitimate customer also requests that a girl bring along her portable typewriter when reporting on the job, since he prefers dictating his work directly to the machine.

There are so many good excuses for writing "Secretarial Services" that the operators of hotel steno pools couldn't be expected to guess reasons that might be shady and the girls encourage this delightful policy of—"See, hear and speak no evil."

One pretty informant who helped give us the lowdown on the high-stepping stenos, showed paycheck stubs proving that she'd worked full time as a hotel stenographer for the last six months. She vowed her take-home pay had never slipped below $300 a week in all that time, although her official salary as a public steno was $75 a week, less taxes.

Whether on legitimate errands or on a play-for-pay assignment, the girls came high. In most hotels, stenographic services go for $6.80 an hour before 5:00 P.M. and soar to $10 an hour for evening rates. If their short-term boss dictates things they never learned in school, the gals collect their *special* fees in cash. It is seldom less than $20, very often $50 and, on especially frolicsome occasions the fee can reach $100.

"We had a Hundred Dollar Club for girls who made that tip," said one of the tattlers on the system. "I never made that, but I got lots of fifties."

She enthusiastically confirmed the fact that Manhattan's better hotels attract the country's biggest spenders, by pointing out that during all her six months service at the hotel, she got only one mild complaint about the prices charged. She had spent a carefree four hours, two of them evening time, with a pinch-penny lover and her personal reward was $50. He apparently thought that covered everything and suffered further pain on his Bromo Seltzer morning-after, when the hotel sent up a bill listing "Secretarial Services—$33.60."

After the fog cleared away, he got a pencil and figured out for himself the actual cost of his lark. It ran as follows:

Secretarial Service 2 hours before 5:00 P.M.	*$13.60*
Secretarial Service 2 hours at evening rates	*20.00*
Secretary's "special" fee	*50.00*
Grand total for a grand evening	*$83.60*

Late the next afternoon, he ran into the dictation doxie and complained. "Look, I really like you a lot, but I need more of a penny ante game—the stakes are too high here."

In the interest of safety, the girl explained to us, getting on the service's "love-with-the-letters" list was difficult for the average man. She said the girls never allowed a man to end his sentences with a proposition instead of a preposition—unless a previous customer they trusted had recommended the new stag.

She said the better hotels and operators of hotel steno pools constantly try to guard against such shenanigans. They employ gents who would check into a room, call for a secretary and then dictate a couple of dummy letters before trying to wangle a wench into an amorous incident that would get her kind tossed out on her round heels. For this reason, the girls seldom take on a stranger . . . So don't get any ideas.

Plenty tried, though. Another girl who helped put this story together described the approach used by three out of four love-hungry executives.

"They wait till the work's over and you're heading for the door," she said. "Then, as they open it for you, they say, 'All my other secretaries always kiss me goodbye.' " She added thoughtfully, "You can be darn sure, if you let him kiss you, it wouldn't be goodbye. But we never do, unless we know them."

Guests of a hotel who hanker for a babe who can do more than spell, are given precise instructions, once their credentials are cleared.

They are told, for instance, that the rules of the house forbid girls taking dictation in a room with the door closed. And on every floor of the hotel there's a floor clerk—usually an elderly woman—whose job includes notifying the security force when that law is being broken.

But for a ten spot when a good-time Charlie moves in, the floor clerk gets wonderfully near-sighted.

However, life isn't all fun for the secretarial sirens, of course. They are usually as expert at their legitimate jobs as they are satisfying in less legal departments. Some can tickle the typewriter keys at the rate of one hundred words per minute and can take shorthand as well. But the prettier a secretary is, the less time she may devote to her Underwood.

As we warned earlier, however, don't run—don't even walk to the nearest hotel to dictate your letters. By no means do all of the girls available through these hotel stenographic services play this game. And those who do, are cautious about the few who buy their favors.

So be careful. One slip could get you slapped—possibly right into the hoosegow.

THE GREAT
GRAIN SWINDLE

A couple of smart Broadway operators rigged a con game to separate the 'down-under' farmers from bushels of their dough and got away with it!

THE TWO AMERICANS sitting in the president's office in the Melbourne, Australia bank looked like hidebound, conservative businessmen. But their proposition sounded so preposterous the banker was about to buzz for a couple of hefty guards.

The two New Yorkers had forty thousand hard-to-get

American dollars, which they wished to deposit in his bank and later give away to Australian wheat farmers. They also wanted to rent several of the city's biggest granaries.

In simple, basic terms, they explained how they wanted to run a contest. An Aussie growing anything from 1 to 10,000 acres of wheat was eligible to enter. He had merely to submit two bushels of what he considered his best wheat, which was to be tested and graded by experts.

The contestant with the best sample was to be rewarded with $25,000 and there were runner-up prizes of $10,000 and $5,000 for second and third place.

Try as he would, the banker could find no loopholes in the plan. Who, he wanted to know, were to be the judges? He himself was invited to head a committee which would appoint them and supervise the entire contest, to see that everything went according to Hoyle. Respectfully, the boys from Broadway also asked him to recommend other prominent business men for the board—and to suggest the country's leading authorities on grain.

They added they'd also like him to approve the ads they'd prepared to run in papers serving the rich wheat-growing states of Western Australia, South Australia and New South Wales. If there was a flaw in the contest, the banker was darned if he could find it.

Why these bloody Yanks wanted to toss $40,000 out the window locating six bushels of the best Australian wheat was something he couldn't understand. But he wasn't going to refuse such a bonanza. He'd be delighted to cooperate to the fullest. The advertisements popped into the papers and the contest was on.

Australia ranks fifth in wheat production (behind Russia, the U.S.A., China and India), but outranks all four other nations in its fondness for a bet. The land where lotteries and bookmaking are both legal took to the grain gamble like a baby to candy.

Big and little farmers—from Newcastle to Perth—packed up their best two bushels and rushed them to the contest. Top agriculture agents found themselves working from dawn till dusk, sampling entries for weight, texture, hardness and polish.

It took less than a month to finish the "wheat stakes." The winners were named in a fanfare of publicity and the Australian banker mentally tipped his hat to his shrewd American cousins. For the seemingly silly contest had drawn a little better than 50,000 entries of two bushels each, *with every entry becoming the property of the promoters!*

As a result of the contest, the New York city slickers had granaries bursting with some 100,000 bushels of the best wheat Australia can grow, worth (as of this writing) 16 shillings, seven pence on the Melbourne exchange—just a little less than two dollars a bushel in American money.

In other words, by dangling a prize of $40,000 the Broadway hustlers collected close to $200,000. Deducting such expenses as granary rentals, wages to the judges and so forth, they had scored a financial coup netting them over $100,000 for a couple of weeks' work—enough to buy more cheesecake than Lindy's could turn out in a million years.

You just can't beat Broadway. From Melbourne to Madagascar, the boys with the lizard shoes and snap-brim Borsalinos are always ahead of the game. They can think up a new twist in less time than it takes you to remember your social security number, and they can parlay that twist into a mound of moolah in nothing flat.

Chinatown's Newest Kick . . .

BOTTLED OPIUM

"The Man With the Golden Arm" didn't tell the full story of the dope menace. What about Yen Shee Suey, the bottled opium that's being peddled in innocent-looking prune juice jugs?

NARCOTICS AGENTS crashed into a dingy room in New York's teeming lower East Side recently, hoping to catch a dope dealer selling his wares.

The pusher was home and he had company—an owl-eyed bop musician and two girls, the youngest only sixteen. The detectives went briskly to work, turning the tiny apartment upside down. But they found no white heroin powder, no hypodermic needle, not even a marijuana cigarette.

The pockets and purses of the suspects produced nothing more in the way of evidence. Though the pusher had a wad of green totaling $368, there was nothing to show how he earned it.

One of the cops was thirsty, so he went to the icebox in the corner of the room and peered inside.

"Nothing but prune juice," he grumbled.

What he didn't know was that the three prune juice bottles were loaded with the drug addicts' newest thrill—bottled opium, known as Yen Shee Suey.

Poets have written about dreams that turn to ashes but Yen Shee Suey is proof that ashes also turn to dreams. An Oriental concoction you won't find listed on the menu of any Chinese restaurant, Yen Shee Suey means Opium Ashes Wine.

To make it, the peddler boils the alcohol out of a bottle of ordinary cooking wine and adds two or three tablespoons of ashes scraped from the bowls of opium pipes. In China, where opium smoking is a national habit, dope dealers are getting richer from the opium ashes they once threw away. Now the ashes are being salvaged—to be used for still another evil purpose—Yen Shee Suey.

When an opium pipe has been smoked several times and the bowl is thickly crusted, the ashes are scraped off for shipment to the United States as medicinal powdered charcoal, which the black stuff closely resembles. Customs inspectors won't realize until they read this that the innocent-looking *charcoal* actually is dream dust.

Prune juice bottles with the original labels intact make the perfect containers for the bottled opium, as it looks like prune juice, smells like prune juice, even tastes like bitter prunes.

Because the prune juice gimmick is new and almost foolproof, unwary detectives pass the bottles by without a second glance during dope raids.

Somewhat less potent than straight opium, heroin or cocaine, Yen Shee Suey is potentially much more dangerous because it is easier to obtain and conceal.

Pushers peddle the bottled opium in the same way as other illicit narcotics, but with little danger of arrest. They simply tell their customers:

"Shake well before serving—and store in a cool place."

A few sips and the drinker blasts off to the intersection of Dream Street and Nightmare Alley.

"We keep Yen Shee Suey handy for the tough times between shots of the real stuff," an addict confided. "It takes the edge off, like a between meals snack. Now that the heat is on, it's hard to buy enough genuine junk to keep us going. And when the monkey is on your back and you can't get a fix, it's murder. That's where opium wine comes in. It's a crutch."

Marijuana smokers love Yen Shee Suey too. It packs more wallop than the joy sticks, with never a cigarette hangover. When the Feds cracked down on the weed-puffers in Broadway's music world, hipsters rapidly made the switch to opium juice. Generally credited with introducing his musical brethren to the bottled opium kick was that great modern jazz saxophonist, Charlie "Yardbird" Parker.

A long-time user of drugs, Parker had tangled with the law on numerous occasions. Narcotics agents watched him like a hawk, but it's an open secret among his intimates that Charlie was on Yen Shee Suey even when the cops were breathing down his neck.

The hopheads say Yen Shee Suey makes dope-taking so cool and easy that even a child can do it. And they do. Many 'teen kick-seekers have tossed away their reefers in favor of the Yen Shee Suey parties. The blue jeans set chip in to buy a bottle and then pass the joy juice around.

The going price for bottled opium in Gotham's Chinatown and elsewhere is about $5 for a 24-ounce jug, and yields enough prune-flavored poppy pop for a dozen high voltage slugs, a dozen dreams in assorted colors.

But just remember this—the Yen Shee Suey addict is hooked just as hard as the snowbird who sniffs cocaine, the hipster who sucks his hop through a pipe stem or the main-liner who bangs home the golden spike!

Like we said before—you can buy anything in New York . . . because she's got a cash box for a heart.

Harlem Hoax . . .

CAFE-AU-LAIT
ON PARK AVENUE

The ebony babes have cooked up a sly stunt to crash Gotham's ritziest nite spots, and get the best tables, too.

IN THE OLD DAYS, Harlem's bronze beauts guzzled their gin in the smoky dives of the black belt, listened to the hot jazz of the Dixieland musicians, and went no further south than the northern fringe of Central Park. It was a Negro heaven then, raucus and noisy, and the uptown crowd worked, lived and played in their own backyard.

Then Dixieland jazz caught on in a big way. Negro musicians like Duke Ellington and Fats Waller and Bunk Johnson, attracted by the lure of cash, began filtering into the little clubs on Broadway, the cellar dives in Greenwich Village, and the hot spots on the East Side.

And when they came, they also brought their dusky dolls with them. The brownskin babes were welcome in these downtown traps where they dined and wined and rubbed shoulders with their white sisters.

But one thing leads to another and soon there were other places these gals longed to go, but couldn't—the glamorous restaurants and glittering nitespots in the East Fifties that you read about in the Broadway and society columns. These were the exclusive domain of the snooty and the snobbish and in some of them the ropes were always up for the colored folk who tried to crash.

But lately something new has been added to the East Side story. Since the United Nations took root in the rocky soil of Manhattan, a swarm of dusky Asian and African delegates, some from newly independent states, became part of the cafe society scene. With the blessing of the State Department, the swarthy diplomats rented apartments in the ritziest East Side areas, began patronizing the best restaurants, and got the bowing welcome, as befits the higher echelon, at the plush nightspots.

And that's when the Harlem chicks saw their chance to invade cafe society's favorite haunts. It all started when a dusky minx learned that the colored foreigners and their ladies were getting the glad-hand welcome at the more elegant nitespots. These were the sluicing parlors which this dusky cutie had been dying to crash for years. And so she pulled a switch which started a trend that is frustrating Gotham's smartest maitre d's.

Here's what she did. Noticing that the Indians, Pakistanis and Africans were being given the open-door policy, our cafe-au-lait doll picked herself up and rented, for a small sum, a sari and forehead jewel, the native costume of India, from a Broadway costumer. Then she got herself a white boy friend to pitch into the plot.

That evening, in her rented sari, and on the arm of her escort, she pulled up in a cab outside one of New York's more swanky nitespots, a rendezvous for cafe society. Draped in the flowing, multi-colored sari, with the star sapphire sparkling in her forehead, our little doll looked and acted the part of Indian royalty.

She swept into the club playing the regal bit to the hilt. The maitre d', not knowing who she was, but thinking she must be someone special, kissed her brown little hand in his suavest continental manner and bowed her to a ringside table. This was something, for a ringside table in this place is reserved for only the creme-de-la-creme and this little cookie was hardly the creme-de-la-creme.

The captain and the waiters were lavish in their attentions and the amused escort found that in the company of a Harlem wench, he finally made it big among the snooty set.

Now the word is out that the gimmick works and the coffee-colored gals with their rented saris, impersonating the genuine Maharanees, are plaguing Park Avenue's exclusive niteclubs and restaurants. The owners are going daffy trying to figure out who's who. Who is visiting royalty, whom they dare not offend—and who is the gal from Harlem?

And one night, if eighteen Indian princesses turn up at the

same time in a posh supper club, who's to decide which ones are the genuine article and which are the ebony cuties just down from 125th Street and Lenox Avenue, whose masquerade party has turned Manhattan cafe society into a crazy-quilt kaleidoscope of color?

Legal Larceny . . .

WANTED . . . 1000 SUCKERS FOR A "SURE THING"

How an oil promoter parlayed a money-back guarantee into a get-rich-quick scheme that the law couldn't touch!

INVEST A HUNDRED dollars in an oil well with a positive guarantee of money back plus a profit? This may seem like a pretty strong statement, but the fact is that if larceny could be made foolproof there'd be a lot of honest people practising it! The late Damon Runyon was fond of remarking that there's a little larceny in the best of us—it just takes the right situation to bring it out.

As a case in point, Runyon would cite the simple situation of what happens when an honest person finds a coin dropped by mistake in the return slot of a public telephone. Not once has such a chance find been returned to the phone company. Since there was absolutely no danger of being caught for stealing, the lucky finder merely pocketed the coin and strolled away.

That, Runyon declared, was a form of legal larceny—the kind of thing everyone looks for, but not everyone finds—clear profit and no risk!

In other words, there's a lot of profit in being crookedly honest. But when you can combine honesty with legal larceny, you're really in. It can be done, too, as was recently discovered by a New York oil promoter.

This glib operator, who needed money to drill a well, advertised in the New York newspapers for 1,000 investors with $100 each. Advertising for investors willing to risk small capital is nothing new. The newspaper columns are full of such ads every Sunday.

But this oil sharpshooter really came up with a gimmick that had people falling all over themselves to cut in. He guaranteed unconditionally that each investor would get his money back in ten years. And if the well came in they would also share in the profits. What could be sweeter!

When other oil men read the ad, they all sat back waiting for the men with the white coats to come along and take the promoter away. Only a guy with a hole in the head, they reasoned, would make a deal like that—guarantee an investor's money back even if the well didn't come in.

The wise hombres in the oil business didn't fall for the bait, but the public did. Within a few weeks the author of the ad had received through the mails, the hundred grand for which he had advertised.

It's no secret that money solicited through the mails receives immediate attention from Post Office sleuths. If any hocus-pocus is found, it can mean an inevitable vacation "up the river." After all, Uncle Sam doesn't like to be made a sucker —nor have any of his agencies used as sucker traps.

Sure enough, authorities microscoped the deal, certain there was something phony. But, to everyone's surprise, they found no basis for complaint, and the nimble-witted oil man emerged as the smartest operator of the generation. His idea was real genius, one that would win a top niche in a hustler's Hall of Fame.

What did he do to keep from being charged with using the mails to defraud?

Well, first of all, he stayed right within the whisker of the law. On receipt of all the money, the oil promoter sent each of his investors a U.S. Government Bond, which he purchased at the market price of $75—but which would be worth $100 when it matured in ten years.

The rest is a matter of simple arithmetic, which you can figure out yourself.

But if you don't want to, here's how it figures: Having received a total of $100,000 from the investors, and having spent $75,000 for the bonds, there was a neat $25,000 left in the promoter's hot little hands.

Meanwhile, back at the well, the twenty-five grand is sunk into drilling equipment, in hopes of tapping a gusher. If it comes in, everyone gets richer. If it doesn't, nobody gets hurt because in ten years, the bonds turned over to the investors will be worth $100 . . . the amount of money each originally invested.

And that, Damon Runyon would admit, is real genius. The kind of honest larceny that would have kept smart swindlers like Ponzi and Yellow Kid Weill from taking a rap if they'd been smart enough to figure it out.

Pretty neat!

The bait that hooked the suckers

"High" Society . . .

CAFE SOCIETY
HAS HATCHED UP
A NEW ONE . . .

If you're the life of the party at 5 a.m., don't think you're suddenly getting younger. Your goofy hostess has probably slipped you a fast one!

"**N**OW IS THE TIME for every good man to come to the aid of the party."

That little phrase, New York style, is more than a test for apprentice typists. And the "party" in question is not Democratic or Republican. It's the sort of percolating potboiling party cooked up by the cunning cuties who make up Manhattan's social sophisticated Cafe Society.

The tablehoppers and brawl-tossers who comprise this carefree coterie are firm believers in coming to the aid of every party they throw. These wingdings aren't the sort of soirees sane folk are used to—a couple of drinks, a few hours of congenial companionship, and then a trip home to sleep.

However, when you hobnob with the hoi polloi and bump elbows with the Tiffany set, the parties are usually all-night affairs. They rarely, if ever, break up before dawn smiles—or frowns, as the case may be—on the proceedings.

The longer they last, the better they are—according to the values of those who go to them. So it's only common logic that a hostess hungry for a high rating will try to keep her guests swinging as long as she can. Her reputation is at stake. Nowadays the hip hostess takes out a pharmaceutical insurance policy. She keeps her party jumping—and the grand prize may well be permanent heart damage or a trip to the morgue for some unwary guest!

It could happen to you any day now. You go to a shindig expecting to bid goodbye to your hostess at around midnight, suddenly glance at your watch and discover it's five in the dawning. What's more, the binge is still going strong. No one acts tired and neither are you.

Wha' hoppen? After all those trips to the bar you should be out on your feet—asleep in a chair. The people are the same ones you've yawned at more than once before. The giggle soup tasted the same. What has you snapping when you should be snoozing? Yet the fact is you're wide awake. You never had so much pep, pop and crackle.

The secret? It's a dangerous new gimmick dreamed up by some goofy party givers who are trying to prove there's no society like "high" society. Completely unbeknownst to you, your host or hostess has been slipping dexedrine in your drinks.

Result? The party keeps roaring—and so do you. It's this powerful stimulant that has you sailing when you ought to be slumbering.

You can't taste it, you can't smell it, but brother—how you feel it!

Just a few grains of the stuff slyly slipped into the drinks will spark a good-sized house party to high jinks you'd scarcely believe. Your screwball hostess knows that half a "dexie" tablet popped in a shaker-full of martinis will turn a smaller soiree into a riot on the rocks. You can't even be safe sticking to Scotch and water, since dexedrine will mingle up a tingle in the most innocent highball, while you remain completely unaware of what's going on.

Bent on tossing the year's most-talked about brawl, these giddy party givers will go to any lengths to get a supply of dexedrine for their refreshments. The drug is not available except by prescription, but many a careless doctor will write one for what he assumes will be normal usage. Our supercharged party sponsors merely save a whole bottle of the tablets for one big blowout.

They conveniently ignore the fact that dexedrine is dangerous, particularly to those of their guests with heart conditions. Combining it with liquor just makes it that much worse.

But as a guest at one of these hep hoedowns, there's nothing much you can do if your hostess wants to play this cute new trick. Since the stuff is undetectable in your drinks, your only tip-off is an exhilarated feeling that makes you want to stay and stay, talk and talk and flirt and flirt. Many a man and woman who'd never dream of using dexedrine have found themselves higher than a kite on the stuff after one of these binges.

And don't be fooled when and if it happens to you. You may *feel* as young as a colt but it won't last.

Bear one other thing in mind, too. What your hostess cannot serve you is a cushion—the kind you'll need when you fall off that pink cloud.

THE CHAIN LETTER— WALL STREET'S NEWEST GIMMICK

A couple of "financial wizards" have come up with a new use for an old gag to bait the unwary investor.

WALL STREET, the nation's financial marketplace, is located within a few square blocks at the southernmost tip of Manhattan. From ten in the morning, until three-thirty in the afternoon, Monday through Friday, the floor of Wall Street's New York Stock Exchange is a bedlam of frantic

finance, where gilt-edge stocks—and some not so gilt-edge—
are bought and sold.

Young order clerks rush back and forth carrying little slips
of paper that can make one man rich and send another to the
poorhouse. Customers' men shout orders back and forth and
huge blocks of stock change hands again and again.

Years ago this scene was the stage where the world's greed-
iest sharpshooters performed and grew rich. But after the
1929 crash put Wall Street in the red, the Securities Exchange
Commission was established to ride herd on financial shenanigans.

One of the main targets of the SEC in recent years has been
the boiler room, the stock swindlers paradise for clipping the
Johnny Babbitts of the suburbs. The boiler room boys located in hole-in-the-wall offices in the City's financial district,
are suave-tongued swindlers whose chief stock-in-trade is
convincing speech and worthless stock. They woo their
suckers strictly by telephone, touting their wares under the
tempting guise of "sure" things, thus mulcting unwary investors out of hundreds of millions of dollars over the past
few decades.

However, the SEC always on the alert, has closed in on
most of these racketeers and has sealed for the time being at
least, the doom of the boiler room. Yes, the SEC does a wonderful job as the watch dog of financial finagling but you
can't keep a smart swindler down, that is, not down on Wall
Street.

Once the law catches up with his racket, he bounces right
back with another like the latest come-on scheme that has
just been cooked up to give certain stocks an illegal shot in
the arm. This new device is a stock market version of the old
chain letter racket designed to inflate the market price of

133

securities, and the way the chumps are falling proves again that a sucker and his money love to waltz in opposite directions.

"How does this dodge work?

It's easy. The guy who whipped it up grabs himself a neat handful of a cheap listed stock, at a depressed price. Then he prepares a chain letter as follows:

```
COPY THIS LETTER WORD FOR WORD AND MAIL OR
  GIVE A COPY TO AT LEAST 10 FRIENDS.

              XYZ For Riches

Buy XYZ CO. common stock from any stockbroker
listed in the telephone book.  Buy as many
shares of XYZ as you can afford.  Try to buy
at least 50 shares.  Then send copies of this
letter to at least 10 friends, nothing else.
Keep XYZ stock and sell it later at a big
profit.  This stock is expected to double in
price quickly.  Please do not break this
chain if you are not able to buy XYZ CO.
stock yourself.  Help your friends to riches
through XYZ by sending them a copy of this
letter.  This is a big company and it is
listed on the stock exchange.  Ask any broker
or bank about XYZ.

    PLEASE DO NOT BREAK OUR XYZ CHAIN!

  REMEMBER!   THE MORE WHO BUY, THE MORE YOU
                    GAIN
```

He mimeographs several thousand copies and mails them by the carload to a list of unsophisticated investors. The letter is minus a signature and a return address and, as you can see, frantically urges the suckers to buy XYZ stock, and in turn to send copies of the letter to 10 friends.

The latter part of the letter, *"Please do not break our XYZ chain,"* is the gimmick the clip artist is counting on. The chain letter routine can have an effect like a snowball rolling down a mountain.

Since Wall Street operates strictly along the lines of supply and demand, when there are more buyers than sellers for a stock, the price jumps accordingly. And when the price jumps high enough, due to the impetus of the chain letter, our friend unloads his bushel basket and cashes in his chips for a neat profit, while the chumps are left holding the bag.

Wall Street—what a marvelous magnet for sucker money!

Deviates' Delight . . .

BOHEMIAN ROULETTE

A tip-off on the bawdy boudoir game Greenwich Village is playing. It's a real gone version of musical chairs, played to the tune of "Anything Goes!"

IT'S QUITE A place. It's the place where the streets are twisted and so are the people. It's the place where the buildings are low and the morals are lower. It's the place where the lady named Manhattan kicks off her shoes, lets down her hair, and goes out of her mind.

It's Greenwich Village.

There's even a block called Gay Street—and it lives up to its name. It's easy to tell the boys and girls apart there. The boys wear dresses and the girls wear pants. What could be simpler? Phony artists and artistic phonies, bearded beatniks and twisted twerps—they're all present, if not accounted for.

Sex is the Village social symbol, and what goes on is more than symbolic. Now the Village oddballs have put a new wrinkle in an old game, and what they've come up with is a new boudoir pastime that has the uptown set giggling in its martinis.

The name of the game is Bohemian Roulette. And, unless you know the rules, taking a peek at a group of guys and dolls indulging in this sassy sport would have you convinced you were watching a maypole dance with innovations.

You have to be real gone to join these gay gambols. Compared to *this* pashy pastime, wife-swapping is like "Spin the Bottle."

Bohemian Roulette got its start a short while back when some of the long-haired boys and short-haired gals with hormones to burn and not a sign of inhibitions got bored with the inevitable routine of romance and decided to introduce an element of guaranteed surprise into the operation of "girl meets boy" . . . "boy meets boy" . . . etc., etc.

A dozen of the mixed-up set—six guys and six gals—are invited to a soiree and, when the gin, bourbon and Scotch are flowing, the merry-go-round maneuver that out-Pollys even Polly Adler, swings into high gear.

All the babes form an inner circle which, at the signal from a waiting pianist, begin to revolve clockwise. As the ladies launch their whirl, the gentlemen walk or dance in a larger circle, outside the femmes, going in the opposite direction. When the pianist stops on a sudden note in mid-song, the gal and guy facing each other grab their partner for a wham, bam, thank you ma'am! If that sounds like "Post Office," mixmaster style, believe you us—it is.

The Village weirdies named this startling sport in honor of Russian roulette, an amusement only slightly more deadly, in which a group of two or more people pass around a revolver with one loaded chamber. Each dimwit takes turns at spinning the chamber, placing the gun to his head and then pulling the trigger.

The diversion continues until someone is "IT," but Bohemian Roulette caught on more rapidly, probably because the chances of getting killed at it were at least a *little* less, and the method of dying—if it came to that—was a good deal more entertaining.

From the very start, the game is enough to make your eyeballs pop. But leave it to the crowd on the freaky fringe to improve on even this bawdy bed-time caper. According to the reports that buzz from table to table in the "artistic" clubs where the deviates roost, the latest version is a slam-bang minuet for those who like to cook with gasps!

The piano player maintains his usual spot, with his back to the players, but the two circles are now composed of both boys and girls, tossed together in a helter-skelter collection. Consider this refinement a moment and you'll see that the results of one of these modernized fandangos can be fantastic.

The maestro strikes up a tune and the players whirl around as diagrammed in this chapter. In Bohemian Roulette, when the music stops a chick may find herself paired with a boy or a babe. The males get the same thing—sometimes the music links them with a lady or a freshly shaved lad. Thus, two and two should be even, but in these amorous antics, it just as often comes out odd—mighty odd.

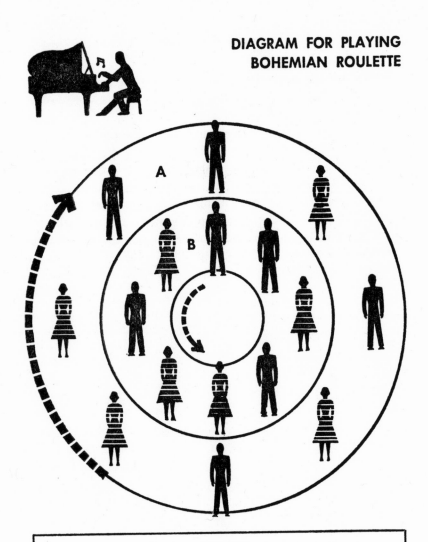

DIAGRAM FOR PLAYING BOHEMIAN ROULETTE

RULES OF THE GAME

1) Music starts with the tune "Anything Goes."
2) When the music begins outer circle (A) goes round and round.
3) At same time, inner circle (B) takes off in opposite direction.
4) Principal rule of BOHEMIAN ROULETTE is to forget all rules!

That doesn't worry the players. During the dance, they're fast on their feet and, when the music stops, they're even faster off them.

As we go to press, the latest of these romps took place in a rented Greenwich Village flat. Don't ask for the address; by the time you're reading these pages, the music will have gone 'round and 'round to come out somewhere else.

We'll give you one tip. The main worry of those who plan one of these whoop-dee-doos is getting the same piano player, a well-known ivory beater. Seems he's in great demand 'cause the guy beats out such an inspired version of *"Anything Goes."*

Haven for Despair . . .

SUICIDES ANONYMOUS

New York, city of heaven and heartbreak, is a mecca for suicides. That's why the voice that answers when you dial Murray Hill 7-2142 has already saved more than fifty thousand lives!

THE GIRL HAD A strange, tense look in her eyes. She was sitting on the edge of the bed holding a telephone in her hand. On the night table was a burning cigarette and an open bottle of sleeping pills.

She dialed the number carefully—Murray Hill 7-2142. It

was three o'clock in the morning, but a voice at the other end answered immediately. The girl's fingers tightened around the phone. She spoke quietly: "I'm going to kill myself."

The anonymous voice was soothing, gentle—and not in the least surprised. "Why?" he asked, as if it was the most normal thing in the world to say. His soothing voice went on: "Every problem can be solved. Let's meet and talk it over."

The girl and the man with the anonymous voice met an hour later in front of the Paramount Theatre in Times Square. They were complete strangers, but for the girl the meeting was a slim thread of hope, a desperate last chance to talk to somebody—anybody—who would listen with sympathy in the big, cold world of New York. For the man, Harry M. Warren of 505 Fifth Avenue, it was one of thousands of would-be suicides who come to him each year for help.

The girl was one of the many who come to New York from small towns looking for the big break. She had gotten pregnant and her boyfriend, whom she had met in Manhattan, was a soldier who was about to be shipped overseas. The problem was "solved" by getting the Army to grant the boy leave, and they were married in Warren's own home, with Warren as best man.

How did the girl find out about Harry Warren and his amazing "Save-A-Life-League?" Warren himself doesn't know—probably on a tip from a doctor, lawyer, or minister.

Harry Warren is a big, gentle, middle-aged man—the son of a Baptist minister who founded "Suicides Anonymous" after he had been summoned to the bedside of a dying suicide and found he might have prevented it by just being available for a talk.

Harry Warren took over the movement after his father's death. Ever since, he has been pitting his human touch against the deep, dark urges that drive people to kill themselves. The men and women who seek him out are of all ages and from all walks of life.

"Every person," says Warren, "thinks of destroying himself at one time or another. But no one really wants to die. Give a person a ray of hope and he'll grab it."

A ray of hope is exactly what "Suicides Anonymous" offers people in despair. No charge is made. All their funds come from individual contributions. The New York office is staffed with several field workers, and has an advisory board of distinguished psychiatrists, ministers, attorneys, and businessmen. Calls come in to the Manhattan office twenty-four hours a day, and mail pours in from everywhere.

In New York alone, fifty people die every day by their own hand—almost twenty thousand a year. More Americans have died by suicide during this century than were killed in both World Wars. They range from the rich and famous, like millionaire Robert R. Young, to the broken-hearted model, and the bum who can't scrounge a meal.

Every time a celebrity dies by suicide, a wave of suicides follows in its wake. A famous woman who killed herself recently caused letters to come into "Suicides Anonymous" like this example: *"She was famous. I am nobody. She was rich. I am poor. She lived an exciting life. Mine is dull. She had everything to live for. I don't. She chose death. So will I."*

What makes despondent people write, phone, and come to Harry Warren and his "Suicides Anonymous?" First, because he is a stranger. He doesn't "remember" names and addresses. He doesn't notify families, employers, or the police.

With Warren, the dreaded secret stops there. You come into his life anonymously and leave anonymously. He removes the fear of exposure or the possible stigma of "insanity." And unlike other similar organizations that help alcoholics and narcotic addicts, there are no inspirational meetings held by "Suicides Anonymous." Every "case" is a brand new one.

Harry Warren's secret weapon is his voice. It doesn't punish or sentimentalize. It calms hysteria and goes into battle with a kindly word, a warm smile, and the confidence that brings trust. These are the only tools he has against the enemy—death.

Once a fifty-year old manufacturer from New York's garment district—tired and dirty from walking the streets all night—came to Warren's office early in the morning. He stood in the doorway defiantly, his clothes wrinkled, his hair uncombed.

"You're not going to stop me!" he flung out at Warren. "I'm going to do away with myself. I just came by to tell you, that's all."

Harry Warren went along with the man's feeling of urgency. "You probably have a good reason to do it," he said. "But I can think of a few why you shouldn't."

The man came a bit closer into the room. "I don't want to hear any bunk—religion and all that."

Warren fought for time. Any delay—for minutes, hours, or days—often works. And Warren knew that suicide threats are not idle. A majority talk about it beforehand.

"Do you play gin?" he asked suddenly. The manufacturer looked at him bewildered. "Yes."

"I have nothing else to do," said Warren. "Neither have you. So let's play a game and talk about what's wrong."

So over a gin rummy game in an office overlooking Fifth Avenue, the dress manufacturer who came out of nowhere sat down with the man from "Suicides Anonymous" in a grim game of life or death. Harry Warren knew what he was do-ing. One of "Suicides Anonymous" most effective maneuvers is to give the despondent person something to do, to steer him away from his one-track obsession.

The manufacturer—who feared his business was going broke—had a long series of talks with Warren before he eventually went back to his home, his family and his business career.

"Suicides Anonymous" has found that well-to-do people kill themselves more often than the poor. The reason: they just can't seem to take the kind of reverses that may change their style of living.

Statistics on suicides remain about the same year after year. A steadily rising rate, three times as many men as women, and over half the total are people between forty and sixty—the "dangerous age." The more educated you are, the more prone to suicide.

According to "Suicides Anonymous," people who work with their hands are less likely to kill themselves than people who do not do manual labor. Negroes rarely commit suicide. The rate is also low for Irishmen.

Love, says "Suicides Anonymous," is only a very minor reason for suicide. The causes are mostly financial, then ill health and domestic difficulties. Although men are in the vast majority, three times as many women actually *attempt* suicide *unsuccessfully*. The women don't really want to die but to attract the pity of a husband or lover and effect a reconciliation.

Easy-going Harry Warren is a shrewd observer of human nature. He's been the target of frauds, but they usually don't get far. Sometimes a call comes in, supposedly from a doctor, saying a patient is coming over to see him. The man ar-

145

rives with a story of poverty, hard luck, and despair. He's angling for a handout of anything over ten dollars, but he could have saved the effort. Warren's intuition about people is unerring.

New York City is a mecca for suicides. The majority are New Yorkers who probably can't stand the "rat-race" of big-city life, but hundreds are out-of-towners who find in Manhattan the ideal conditions—obscurity, high places to jump from, and no interference from friends and relatives.

The only man in New York who is standing by to help them, if they want help, is the anonymous voice that answers when you dial Murray Hill 7-2142.

Hats, Coats and Cuties

TIP-OFF ON NEW YORK HAT-CHECK GIRLS

When a fedora filly was arrested on a morals charge, she had this to say: "You'll never know what that job—hat checking, I mean—did to my feet!"

IF 1960 MATCHES years gone by, nearly 50,000 pert, pretty kids—from the corn cribs of Ohio, the cotton fields of Alabama and points in between—will enlist in that curvaceous army, the Manhattan hat-check brigade. Probably not one of that number is aware of the grim odds against her. These are the mathematical chances of a hatchick turning into a call girl.

It's exactly five times more likely to happen than with the girl who decides to prance in a chorus line, twelve times more probable than with those who decide to become secretaries, and a whopping thirty-one times more likely than for the average, run-of-the-mill girl.

These facts are no reason for hat-chicks to form protest parades down Broadway. We want to *emphasize* that not *all* of them turn to cuddling for coin. Certainly not the majority! But we'd like to ask Dr. Kinsey, if he were alive, why so many check their morals after a few years of checking hats.

We remember that some of the prettiest dolls ever to grab a fedora in Manhattan were involved in the notorious Minot "Mickey" Jelke vice investigation, which spilled all over New York nightlife. Men who'd cherished their toothy smiles when they passed them their hats, were stunned to learn they'd been plying a more ancient trade between stints at the hat rack.

More than half of the gilded doxies who took the stand in that shocking trial had served time as hatchicks in some of New York's plushiest spots.

What makes her do it, this clean-cut kid from the sticks who would have slapped the face of a boy in her home town who even suggested such a fate? In general, she's a dreamer. She takes that job thinking she'll make nice money, meet lots of celebrities, and maybe captivate a millionaire into leading her to the altar.

What reality gives her, instead, isn't so nice. She stands on her feet eight hours a night, five nights a week, for anywhere from $38 to $50 per week, in the top spots, and considerably less in the second and third-rate dives. In a popular club, she'll wrestle an average of three hundred topcoats or overcoats on and off customers every night.

At about five pounds of weight per garment, and that's light, it means she hauls and hoists better than one ton of wool every working night. For this, she's trading her youth (age eighteen is preferred and thirty-five is out in this business), as well as her good looks (choice places actually *audition* girls for their vacancies).

While she's developing muscles a bantam-weight boxer might envy, Miss Hatchick begins to take note of situations around her which would bring out the green dragon in a saint. Night after night, girls no prettier than she swirl past in clouds of expensive perfume, wrapped in minks ten years of hat-check wages wouldn't buy.

The club's gossip circuits quickly give her the low-down. That haughty blonde with the glittering diamond necklace is the mistress of a steel millionaire who can't spend his money fast enough. The beautiful brunette who collects pearl chokers like kids collect stamps is the girl friend a big dress manufacturer goes home to, instead of his wife.

The way those dolls are living isn't legal, but it looks mighty exciting, as well as profitable, to a kid who has to make a choice between going to a movie or having dinner on her night off, because she can't afford both. When the propositions start coming, they're tough to turn down, because they're voiced by the very same men who are taking such luxurious care of the sweeties the hat chick has come to envy.

Meantime, what about those golden dreams she started with? One actually does come true. She meets celebrities, all right, every night of the year. She even reaches the stage where she gives them a personal, "Good Evening," and gets a return greeting. She soon learns, however, that notables careful of their reputation go no further, and those who pause to whisper sweet nothings are up to no good.

One hatchick's diary had dozens of entries which will give you an idea: The Hollywood movie star who picked her for a two-hour romance, and gave her $20, instead of the $50 she had expected, or the Broadway producer who invited her to a swank Manhattan hotel, let her sit around two hours and—when no big urge overcame him—sent her home with $5 for the cab.

The club where a hatchick works has thought way ahead of her about that millionaire she'd like to meet and maybe marry. Her employer has a rule she can't mingle with the customers—at least not in the place where she works. She can meet a date someplace else, but remember, she's working five nights a week until 3:00 A.M. and the only spots left at that hour are the all-night hamburger joints and a few scattered all-night bottle clubs, mainly in Harlem or Greenwich Village.

If she has any brains, she skips the latter, because the average man who's been sluicing down giggle soup until just before dawn *cannot* be guaranteed even to stay on his feet, much less his good behavior, in the hours that follow.

If the hatchick decides to duck the rumpot playboy who keeps her kind of hours—to bed at dawn and up again at 4:00 P.M.—her choice of companions usually narrows down to a musician in the place where she works or an out-of-work youth with ambitions—but nothing else—to burn.

Let's also dispense with that pipe dream of being suddenly discovered by a talent scout and lifted, overnight, from a gal who checks minks to one who wears them. We talked to a half a dozen men who hire the majority of New York's hatchicks and not one of them could recall a single example of hat-check-girl-becomes-starlet.

Don't get the idea from what we've said, so far, that this hat-check business belongs in the penny-ante league. Conservative estimates are that more than $5,000,000 is paid out yearly by big city restaurants and nightclub patrons, merely for the privilege of reclaiming their own hats and coats and wearing them home.

Many a lush nightspot has actually been launched on money paid out for the hat-check concession. And there's hardly a bistro boss in New York who won't admit that this side swag was all that kept him going over the lean years.

Consider a few examples of the "take": One of New York's big Broadway niteclubs is reliably reported to get $55,000 for its hat-check concession and another nets $50,000. Scale that down to the hundreds of small restaurants getting $150 per week for the same service and it's plain this is income with a capital "I."

With all that cash floating around, a hat-check kid would be less than human if she didn't try to get a little for herself. She soon learns she's on a salary, period! She gets absolutely no split or percentage of the normal quarters, halves and dollars she takes in as tips. She's not even allowed a slice of anything up to five dollars. If a playboy's generosity should go beyond that—and it's a red letter day when it occurs—the hat-chick is allowed to keep *half* of everything over a five spot. On a $20 tip, for example, her extra gravy is $7.50.

Lest she be tempted to steal, there are all sorts of handicaps put in her way. First and foremost, she gets a pretty little uniform which has no pockets, for an obvious reason. Next, she's placed on duty with another girl who may be her friend

151

or may be tipping off the boss, if she tries keeping the change once too often.

If her partner and she really become good friends, their jobs are switched and a stranger goes in as a replacement. To top it off, "spotters" go around redeeming their hats with marked coins and dollar bills. Woe to the hat chick, if the marked money doesn't show up in the night's receipts.

As for the schemer who tries to invent a fool-proof method of "skimming it off the top," as the trade calls a little gentle stealing, she's always told about the hatchick with the itchy neck. It seems this smartie used to collect a customer's quarter and then scratch her neck, meantime dropping the coin she'd palmed down her blouse, where it was eventually trapped by a tight belt.

She was also trapped one night, while walking out jingling like Santa's reindeers. After this inventive kid was fired, high and tight necklines became a must in hatcheck uniforms.

Does it all mean there's no such thing as straight-shooting hat-check girls? Not at all. Plenty play it honest. Some use their salaries to pay the room rent, while the folks back home help with the money for dramatic coaching or singing lessons. Some few are happily married and would call their husky husbands if you so much as twitched an eyebrow.

As for the others, well, *you* be the guy to throw the first stone if a girl's tempted after lugging a ton of wool around night after night, while a sly character waves two weeks' rent in her face for "just stopping by the house for a drink some night, baby."

When one of these fedora fillies was recently arrested on a prostitution rap, she had this to say: "I guess you'll think I'm cynical, but you'll never know what that job—hat checking, I mean—did to my feet!"

So, like we said at the start, these are the mathematical chances of a hatchick turning into a call girl. It's exactly five times more likely to happen than with the girl who decides to prance in a chorus line; twelve times more probable than with those who decide to become secretaries, and a whopping thirty-one times more likely than for the average, run-of-the-mill girl.

The Awful Truth . . .

NOW YOU CAN GET THE GOODS ON YOUR WIFE FOR $10.50

You've heard of fingerprints . . . now there's a sneaky new modus operandi to nab wifey with fanny-prints!

DOCTOR KINSEY was the first to put in cold print the fact that nearly half the nation's married women skylark with guys other than their husbands sometime in their lives.

But even if he'd never written a line about it, there are plenty of hubbies who had—and have—their suspicions.

Their trouble, till now, was that there wasn't much the average guy could do about it when he suddenly got that feeling that wifey might be playing around.

He couldn't give up his job and become a Mickey Spillane, skulking around corners to see where the better half was going. And the cost of private eyes, at fees ranging up to one hundred dollars a day, wilt all but the fattest bank accounts.

But the wizards of the test tubes have come up with an easier solution that may soon have many a bounce-around bride ducking for cover. What's more, it's within the price range of even the most humble wallet.

Fluorescent paste, it's called, an odorless, colorless salve that's completely invisible to the naked eye—except when viewed under an ultra-violet light; also known as "black light". Then, something as weird as Merlin's magic happens. The stuff comes to life and glows like a naughty deed in a good world.

Our state department used it for years to coat top-secret files. Let an unauthorized person so much as touch something that was none of his business and the combination of fluorescent paste and the "black lamp" gave him away. It didn't take bright brains long to figure out another use for it . . . nabbing a mama up to monkey business, or a papa, too, for that matter.

Now all Joe Doaks has to do to relieve his mind, or learn the worst, is to buy an ounce of the stuff; cost $1.50. His next and last investment is to get an ultra-violet flashlight; cost $9.00.

Like most worried husbands, he has a good idea who the light of his life might be cheating with. The paste can be used anywhere, but the amateur investigator's best bet is his suspect's car. The odds are overwhelming that the cut-up couple are using it to speed to their rendezvous.

For that matter, you'd be surprised how popular the back of an auto still is for amorous antics. So, seizing his first opportunity, hubby lightly rubs the seats of the suspected interloper's car with the fluorescent paste.

There's nothing to see after the job's done, but the doubting husband now has an invisible cop working for him, full time. When wayward wifey snuggles up to her out-of-bounds boy friend, she doesn't know it, but she's getting fanny-printed. The telltale paste rubs off on her clothing.

If he's right in his hunch that baby's being bad, hubby will have the proof soon enough. All he need do is wait until the little woman's out shopping, or asleep, and turn that ultraviolet light on her duds. The evidence will shine out—the invisible paste on her clothes will glow under the black light.

Incidentally, it's not easy to remove the paste; even a trip to the cleaners won't take all of it out.

Now the missus really *is* in a jam. A series of seemingly harmless questions about where she's been and who she's seen lately quickly settles the issue—but good. If she fibs and claims she hasn't done a thing but go to the super-market and play bridge with "the girls," daddy's got her cold and she has some tall explaining to do.

So here's a word of advice to those high-flying lads who think they're getting off scot-free in an adventure with someone else's spouse. Don't be too sure of yourselves, boys. You may be letting yourself in for a real pasting—in more ways than one.

Tip to—
VISITING FIREMEN

Think you know the difference between a chippie and a lady? Well, the next time you come to the Big Town for a big time, beware the lady in distress!

MANHATTAN IS THE Mecca for the traveling man. The big town calls itself the convention capital of the world—and does its best to live up to the name. Gotham boasts the world's finest restaurants, the most exciting night life, and the nation's most glamorous dolls.

But you've got to be careful on that last score. If you come to town with money to burn, the chances are strong that *you'll* get burned!

You traveling salesmen, business men and convention-goers—especially you guys who seek out a little female diversion while on the loose in New York—beware! Those enterprising Broadway cuties have come up with a neat new racket to separate you from your dough. And the standard B-girl routine is petty larceny in comparison to this new wrinkle.

At least with the B-girls you know the score. You have only yourself to blame if you nibble at their bait and wind up minus your wad. But with this new trap, it's different.

You're dealing with "ladies."

Here's how it works. You're in the big town on business. Since you're traveling on the boss, you're staying at one of the better hotels, which is where these "ladies" operate. The rates are high and a traveling man staying there is apt to be carrying a sizeable bankroll.

Operating time for these gals is around midnight or later, when the streets are fairly empty. It's just about this time that you're returning to your hotel—worn out after a business dinner or, more likely, discouraged at your dateless evening.

As you approach your hotel, you notice two well-dressed ladies—obviously not the "pick-up" type. Suddenly, though, you notice that one of them has doubled up in pain, moaning. The other is solicitously bending over her. The bait is out.

"Please, sir," the well one pleads, "will you help me? I hate to ask a perfect stranger but I have no choice. My friend here has taken ill, and I can't handle her alone. If you could just help me get her home in a taxi, it's only a short ride, I . . ."

She need go no further. It's obvious that she's a lady—perfect speech, perfect dress—and, a lady in distress. Without hesitation, your knightly gallantry comes forward. Within minutes the three of you are in the back seat of a cab—you in the middle. The driver has been given something for an address, and you're on your way.

You've barely rounded the first corner when the healthy one starts getting amorous. This is more than you bargained for. You figure she's just grateful—and besides wasn't a true knight always rewarded for his gallant deeds? Blessing your unexpected luck, you begin enjoying your reward for all it's worth.

Your attention is so completely and enjoyably occupied by this time that you don't even notice that the sick lady on the other side of you has made a remarkable recovery.

While you're happily engaged, so to speak, *she's busily disengaging you from your wallet!*

All too soon for you, you arrived at your destination. "Tell the cab to wait," says your friend. "Just help me inside the door with her."

Still the gallant knight, you do as she requests—stalled from any further pleasures that evening by the promise of a date for the following day—"when we can be alone."

Humming to yourself, you get back in the cab and head for your hotel. You don't stop humming until you get to the hotel and reach for your wallet to pay the cabbie. Too late, you find you've been taken—but good. Dashing back to the address where you dropped the pair is a waste of time—it was a phony. Nobody there ever heard of them. The "ladies" beat it fast—with your wallet—as soon as your cab was out of sight.

Yours is no isolated case, if that be any comfort to you. It's being pulled every day on visiting firemen in New York and more and more of the chiseling chippies are taking up the new racket.

Moral: If you want to be a gentleman and help ladies in distress, fine—but don't get into a cab with them!

159

Mail Cheats . . .

CHISELERS ARE USING
THE U.S. MAILS FOR FREE

The petty larceny boys have dreamed up a slick little scheme to mail their letters without stamps—and the Post Office is delivering them too!

THE POST OFFICE DEPARTMENT hasn't the slightest idea what's going on, but it's being neatly bilked—to the tune of hundreds of thousands of dollars yearly—by sharpies using the U.S. mails for free. You, as a taxpayer, foot the bill.

Duping Uncle Sam into becoming a free messenger boy for your billet doux? On the surface, it doesn't even seem remotely possible. Yet it happens every day, thanks to a post office policy ironically set up to foil the cheats.

The regulation states that letters—or packages—dropped in a mail box with no postage on them are to be promptly returned to the sender. Sounds eminently fair and sensible; foolproof, too.

But don't under-rate the cheats. They've come up with a neat little scheme that makes use of this very rule to mail letters that are delivered without so much as a penny's worth of stamps on them.

Like any other blueprint for larceny, this one is a model of simplicity. The working ground is the envelope of the letter to be mailed. Two important changes are made, however.

Let's say, for the sake of example, that Joe Doakes wants to send a free-riding message to his friend, Sam Jones. Here's what he does.

In the middle of the envelope—where one would normally put the name and address of the person to whom the letter is being mailed—Joe puts *his own name and address*. In the upper left-hand corner, where you or I would place our return address, Joe writes in Sam Jones' name and address.

Let's see what happens after that.

Deposited in a regular corner postbox, Joe's letter is scooped into a bag by the mail collector and taken to a substation, where some clerk notes it has no stamp on it. Automatically, the letter is pulled out from the rest of the mail and marked for return to the sender.

Remember something, though. The name and address in the return corner of this letter is Sam Jones', the man for whom the letter is intended.

Dumped into the proper mail bag, the letter is "returned" all right—but to Sam Jones, the very person wise guy Joe wanted to send it to in the first place. The letter has been delivered for free!

Sam reacts as you or I would when he sees his own name and address in the return corner. He rips the envelope open to find out what goes on and finds a letter—from pal Joey.

Doakes could have used the same gimmick to mail a package, too.

The swindle is limited in its scope. It cannot be employed to send a letter or package out of town—from New York to Chicago, for instance.

Locally, though, it works smooth as silk, so much so that one gyp artist—a Manhattan businessman—recently used the gimmick to mail out no less than one thousand circulars to his best customers. He put nary a stamp on even one of the envelopes. They were all "returned" to the names in the upper left-hand corners—the very people he wanted his circulars to reach.

Penny ante stuff? Sure, in any one individual case. But with enough cheaters taking advantage of this slick dodge, it is costing the Post Office—and the taxpayers—a mint.

Bear in mind that it costs your Uncle Sam far more to go to the bother of returning a piece of mail than it does to deliver a properly addressed letter.

If the Postmaster General is listening, though, there's a way to put an end to his neat little swindle. All he has to do is order his boys in gray to *deliver* letters and packages with no stamps on them—and collect from the addressee. The sharpshooter would find himself forced to pay for everyone of his missives—all delivered to him.

The grafter pulling this gyp on a larger scale would have to answer some embarrassing questions from the postal inspectors. How come he's suddenly getting so many letters with no stamps on 'em?

In the meantime, there's not a thing your postman can do about the free mail scheme. All he's paid to do is deliver the mail, through rain, through sleet, snow and hail—even for the chiselers.

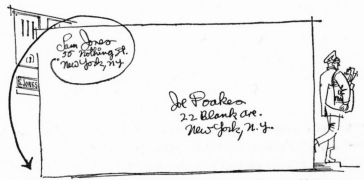

There is no stamp on this letter, so the Post Office would return it to Sam Jones—the very man Joe Doakes wanted it sent to...

Men in White . . .

INSIDE THE "DEATH CONFERENCE"

The secret verdict of his fellow doctors: "Guilty of professional manslaughter!" But you will never hear about it ... nor will this surgeon ever stand trial.

BEHIND THE SOUNDPROOF doors of a private conference room in a New York hospital, a nervous doctor describes his case. Facing one of the most remarkable gatherings of top-flight surgeons ever called into consultation, he has good reason to be jittery.

No suffering emperor stricken with a mysterious ailment ever was attended by such a galaxy of specialized medical talent. Yet the operation they are considering is just an appendectomy; the patient, only an obscure young girl from New York's lower East Side.

Five thousand dollars would not pay the combined total of their usual consulting fees for the hour they will spend. Yet not one of them will render a bill.

You will never learn what really took place behind those sound-proofed doors. Yet what the doctors learn there may some day save your life.

Unhappily, it cannot help the girl in the case; she has already had her operation—and died of it. Even more unhappily, the pathologist's post-operative examination revealed absolutely nothing wrong with her appendix.

Then why was the fatal appendectomy performed? Did the doctor bungle the operation as well as the diagnosis? What really happened? And why did this unfortunate youngster die?

Closeted in the privacy of their death conference, the New York specialists are probing for the answers.

The inquiry was touched off when the pathologist's disturbing post-operative report alerted the Tissue Committee—the group of doctors responsible for looking into everything that comes out in the hospital's operating rooms. Shortly afterward, the operating surgeon received an "invitation" to attend the next "mortality meeting" and explain why and how he performed the surgery that ended so disastrously.

This isn't the kind of invitation a doctor can decline, nor the kind of audience he can hope to fool. Yet the most inept bungler, facing the inquiry with the certainty that what he did is sure to be condemned, has one comforting reassurance: No matter how miserably he handled the case, his fellow doctors will cover up for him.

Privately, they may convict him of professional manslaughter. But publicly you will never hear a whisper that might put him on trial for any of his buried mistakes.

Even in the privacy of the death conference, the procedure is polite and formal. The surgeon presents his case almost as if he seeks advice for a patient whose life might still be saved. He reports every symptom he observed; every test he made; his decision to wait twenty-four hours; his alarm when, despite ice packs, the girl's condition grew worse; his advice to her anxious parents that further postponement of an operation risked death from a ruptured appendix.

Then, step by step, from the first incision to the last stitch, the surgeon describes the operation; his shocked discovery that the appendix was normal; how, after removing it, he explored further and found the real mischief-maker. An important gland, newly active in the budding change of child to woman, had become the center of an angry inflammation.

Could he have known this before he operated? Did he do the right thing after he discovered it? The specialists will cross-examine the operating surgeon about the technical details of everything he did or failed to do. In the end, they will know whether he behaved correctly or whether he completely botched the case.

They will know. But you and I will not. Even the girl's own family will never know whether she died in spite of her surgeon's care—or because of it!

This isn't the only case the doctors have come to hear. Before this death conference adjourns, five or six other doctors may be called to explain, if they can, the unexpected fatalities that followed questionable operations performed in this New York City hospital during the preceding month.

Every major department of this hospital will hold a similar meeting. And no one will ever know how many of the deaths investigated are proven to be needless and inexcusable.

Only doctors are admitted to mortality meetings—and they won't tell. No official record of the proceedings is kept. If a record existed, you would not be allowed to see it. If, somehow, you managed to obtain a transcript, it is doubtful whether any court in the land would accept it in evidence!

Why the secrecy? Because the death conference is for the protection of the hospital—not for the protection of the public. It isn't to prevent the bungling surgeon from killing you; it's to prevent his doing so in their hospital. Because the hospital with a high mortality rate gets a black eye, and that hurts every doctor who practices there.

So if the death conference finds a surgeon unfit to wield the healing knife, the only punishment they demand is his resignation from the hospital staff. He remains free to continue his butchery, so long as he does it somewhere else!

Death conferences held monthly, a practice in many New York hospitals, are a good thing. They help to bring us better medicine by discouraging unnecessary operations; by reducing carelessness; by revealing errors and preventing their repetition; by making available to other doctors the priceless experience and counsel of the best men in every field.

Let's agree that a medical man's professional acts can best be judged by his fellow doctors; that some mistakes are inevitable. But are doctors alone privileged to decide how many such mistakes shall be forgiven? That not one of them shall be acknowledged?

Secrecy is not the way to end the gnawing doubts each one

of us has felt when a loved one's hospital stay ended in unexpected death. Was it really unavoidable?

"Everything possible was done." No doubt. Everything possible except, perhaps, barring the operating room to men whose record proved they were unfit to work there.

Today's death conference is too late to help the victim of yesterday's operation. But it can save tomorrow's if doctors will refuse to go on withholding the identity of the bungler who buries too many mistakes. Which is why the death conference—a procedure in many New York hospitals—is another step forward in saving lives . . . maybe your life.

**Memo to Little
Red Riding Hoods . . .**

SEDUCTION BY
PRESCRIPTION

**The two-legged wolves have found a
new use for a popular pill that makes
babes "relax and enjoy it."**

Fʀᴏᴍ ᴛʜᴇ ꜱᴛᴏɴᴇ ᴀɢᴇ down through the jazz age, the two-
legged wolf has always had a little edge going for him in
perennial pastime. When sex first reared its fascinating head,
the cave man staked out his cutie, belted her over the noggin
with his club, and dragged her to his favorite rock.

The modern lover loaded his babe with booze until she was too drunk to remember, or too sick to care.

Today, Manhattan's lover boys, the suave men-about-town, mix sex with medical science—and the results have been proving most startling. You too can be a successful lover. All it takes is a "harmless" little pill.

This is no secret aphrodisiac or witches' compound. It's a pill which is being sold by the millions in drug stores from coast to coast and all it requires is a doctor's prescription. You've probably taken them yourself.

They're the tranquilizer pills which are manufactured under many different trade names and are prescribed for frayed nerves or slight mental disorders. In some sets they are known as "don't-give-a-damn" pills.

The reaction to one of these little tablets is almost like a brainwash. Tension slackens, nerves loosen, and you find yourself looking at the world through rose-colored glasses.

There are seldom any arguments because nothing seems important enough to argue about.

The ingenious nitelife wolf wasted no time in uncovering the possibilities of this new wonder drug, only he *reversed* the procedure. When he wants a little peace of mind, he doesn't take the pill himself—he gives it to his date. And in about as much time as it takes to polish off a Martini, the doll finds herself in a languorous, lazy state of relaxation.

At this point the babe has become completely submissive and before she realizes it, she is heeding the words of an old philosopher who once said, "When rape is inevitable, relax and enjoy it."

The 1961 wolf is no longer the fast-talking promoter who has to rely on such corny routines as, "How about coming up to see my etchings?" Now he is a solicitous fellow with a bedside manner. The new line is, "Baby, you look tired. I've got just the thing to pick you up."

Then he reaches into his pocket for the little tranquilizer pill and it's not long before he becomes the master.

Since the therapeutic value of this drug has been proven and widely accepted, the gal will gulp her pill with the same assurance she would have if she took an aspirin. When the guy starts to move in, the dame finds that her defenses are down.

She's just too relaxed to struggle, and the modern Svengali adds another victory to his score.

Science marches on!

171

TV Gyp . . .

TELEVISION'S LATEST TALENT RACKET

If you should get a letter inviting you to act on TV, throw it away . . . it's the newest form of sucker bait!

THE POSTCARD OR letter is the most exciting thing the mailman has brought in years. "Dear Sir or Madame," it says, "you have been tentatively selected for a role in a television production by XYZ Studios."—or someting like that. It then goes on to advise you to report at such and such a studio on such and such a date for a film test.

Little old you a television player? Seems incredible. Why, you never acted on the stage in your whole life. Oh yes, you did. You were one of the thousands who made an appearance on one of the many TV audience participation shows that are so popular these days. You got quite a charge when the M.C. announced your name and home town. Remember?

Well, this is how come you received that postcard. The offer is tempting. If you're like a lot of gullible chumps, you reach for the phone, call the number on the postcard, and a honey-sweet voice makes an appointment.

But if you keep the date, mark yourself down as a first-rate sucker. You've just joined the ranks of many who've been mulcted by a TV racket now mushrooming in New York.

Like most dodges, the scheme is disarmingly simple on the surface. All it calls for is a few smart operators to set up a so-called "independent" television production company. When you show up for your screen test, protesting that you never acted in your life, they insist you're just the kind of talent they're hunting for. Hadn't they seen you on TV for a few minutes when you were on that participation show? You projected—"exactly the screen personality they were looking for."

You're ushered to a microphone and handed a script. Built in a wall in front of you is a glass-enclosed control booth where a man fiddles importantly with knobs and dials. You read your lines. Well, what did you expect? You're wonderful! Just made for a part in an upcoming production.

There's one slight hitch, though. You'll have to have a union card. But the genial director who's led you through your test can help with that, too. Quickly, he scribbles a name and address where you can get the card. Frequently, it's conveniently in the same building.

Now all you have to do is pay your union initiation fees and you're on your way to fame and fortune. Fifty dollars, one hundred dollars, the "union" has sliding fees that seem almost geared to your wallet. They'll take as little as you can spare as a down payment on your work card. Why not?

This "union" happens to be as phony as the outfit that sent you there! And that's how the fast-talking gents latch on to your loot.

If you're simple enough, you shell out and then wait for your golden moment before the camera. That's all you do—wait and wait and wait. There are production tie-ups, delayed schedules, trouble with the script and so on—until even the most persistent chump goes away quietly to lick his wounds.

Housewives, salesmen, stenographers, school girls and even children are being rooked right and left for "union fees" that brought them not a smidgin of work.

These glib swindlers operate so brazenly that they even use the phone book for new sucker bait. A man in a wheel chair received a letter telling him a talent scout had spotted him as a vigorous, handsome possibility for one of their shows.

A mother got a letter expressing interest in her boy as a child actor. Obviously XYZ Studios was unaware that her only son was a grown man with three children of his own.

Only a few months ago, a legitimate union, estimated that phony outfits like "XYZ" and a dozen others had already reaped a larcenous harvest of more than $1,000,000 and are still on the loose.

If you get a letter inviting you to become a TV actor because you were seen on TV, by all means dump it in the wastebasket. Chances are the only opportunity you're being offered is to part with your money.

THE REAL STORY
BEHIND AN AD!

Proving that in Gotham's Cafe Society Truth can be Stranger Than Fiction!

IN CAFE SOCIETY money is the root of all evil and adulthood is frequently synonymous with adultery.

The game in the Big Town is played with a vengeance, with wife and hubby cheating on each other like mad—and working like galley slaves to catch the other in the act. The Park Avenue ladies are quick to put the knife in the back of an errant spouse, and their passion for revenge is undying.

It even reaches beyond the grave.

Think we're kidding? Take a peek at the following ad, which appeared word for word in a leading New York newspaper not too long ago:

FOR SALE—*'60* CADILLAC *conv., $50.00 Write Box 242, 1400 Broadway, New York.*

A year-old Caddy convertible for sale for fifty bucks—was this really on the level? The only answer, of course, was to rush a telegram to the box number to request a look at the "bargain."

We got a telephone call in reply and made an appointment to examine the car. That's how we met the gal who'd placed the ad. At once she suggested we have a look at the Cadillac, which was garaged near-by.

We took the buggy for a test spin, found it in perfect condition and came up with two twenties and a sawbuck to clinch the deal. The babe obligingly wrote out a bill of sale and signed the registration over to us.

But that couldn't be the end of it. We had to satisfy our curiosity. Why was she selling a '60 Cad for fifty bucks when any dealer in the world would have given her four grand for it?

"You're not alone in finding it hard to believe," she told us.

She went on to say that two other newspapers had turned her down cold when she offered them the ad. "I guess they thought it preposterous," she said. "But it makes perfect sense to me."

It seems her wealthy playboy husband had kicked the bucket just a few months earlier. The will he left was a cutie . . . in it he expressly ordered her to sell the Cadillac and hand over the proceeds of the sale to his secretary—who had been "so very kind to him."

Instead of fighting the will, the wily widow decided she'd comply with the will to the letter. So she sold the $4,000 Cadillac alright—but *only* for $50.00 and turned over the $50.00 to the "very kind" secretary.

Smart? Natch! That's sophisticated New York.

One for the T-Men . . .

PASSING THE GREEN

The phony money pushers are at it again. Now they have figured out a loophole for unloading counterfeit bills that's almost legal!

I F ANYONE TRIED TO convince you there's a *legal* way to pass counterfeit money, you'd tell him to have his head examined.

But it is true!

Right now, in New York City, a gang of "queer shovers," as the boys are called in the trade, are giving Broadway's restaurant owners a headache with a legal loophole that's a dilly.

The originator of this devious dodge is believed to be an ex-con known to the underworld as Willie the Weeper, who heads up a mob of passers that prey on soft-hearted restaurant owners and managers.

Dressed like a bum, the "Weep," or one of his mob, goes into a restaurant and seeks out the owners. They know from long experience that restaurant owners are easy touches for hungry men, so the passers give the intended victim a hard-luck story about being hungry. Sometimes, just to make it look good, the passer will even offer to work out the price of a meal. That's usually the clincher.

Nine times out of ten, the proprietor will fall. Then after he's had the free meal, the passer pulls his pitch. Going up to the guy who's just been good enough to keep him from dying of hunger, the passer casually pulls a handkerchief from his pocket and deliberately allows a twenty dollar bill to drop to the floor.

When the Samaritan sees this he invariably blows his top and grabs for the "bum's" money. While the latter stands by in pretended dismay, the owner angrily deducts the price of the meal and, after handing back the change, orders the bum out—only to discover later that the double sawbuck he so eagerly reached for is a worthless counterfeit!

And, even if he catches up with the bum later, there's absolutely nothing he can do about it—because, technically, the bum didn't pass the phony money . . . *The restaurant owner passed it on himself!*

You'd be surprised how many business men have fallen—and are still falling—for this trick.

Hundreds of others are taken in by an equally simple dodge. It's not as legally-foolproof, but the passer has the gimmick down so pat that he's usually miles away before the sucker discovers he's been taken.

The passers like to work it around places like Manhattan's busy supermarkets and movie theatres. Supermarkets are an especially favored target, particularly on Saturdays when lines of impatient shoppers queue up. Making a few small purchases, the passer pays for them with a legitimate ten dollar bill. In most cases he gets a five dollar bill back as part of his change.

Then, going through the motions of counting it, he offhandedly asks the busy cashier to change the five into five singles. Without giving it a second thought, the cashier makes the change and drops the five-spot into her cash drawer.

Naturally, she assumes it's the five she just handed out.

It isn't!

What the swindled cashier put into the drawer is a phony five dollar bill, which the passer had palmed in his hand earlier —and which he passes over after quickly stashing the genuine five dollar note she has given him!

Simple? It sure is. And it works in ninety-nine out of one hundred cases because the swindler knows how to prey on human nature. Movie cashiers time after time fall for this same corny larceny and the passer usually is smart enough never to work the same area too often. Sometimes, however, they get greedy and then are suddenly surprised to feel a tap on the shoulder and find themselves face-to-face with a T-man.

If you're handling money take a tip from us: unless you want to be taken, keep your eyes open for the guys who shove the queer. Their phony dough may be green, but definitely— *they're not!*

What you never knew about the "Finest" . . .

PITY THE NEW YORK COP

From the day he joins the Force, the man in blue has plenty to be blue about. Here are the facts and don't be too shocked!

CROOKS HATE HIS guts, so his life is in jeopardy twenty-four hours a day. He faces injury or sudden death every waking moment, yet when you need help he's as close as the sound of your voice or the nearest telephone. For all this, the man in blue in New York's 'Finest' gets paid less than the average taxi driver! Worse still, he's almost always in hock, a situation that starts from the very moment that he is appointed to the Force.

Though he's a member of the 'Finest,' when it comes to giving him a break New York's officialdom is always looking the other way. And it looks like nothing will be done about it until the average citizen wises up to what it costs a cop to be a cop.

From the day he forks over his one dollar filing fee to take his Civil Service Exam that will qualify him for his job, the man who protects your life, property, and children is banging his head against an economic stone wall. Instead of a career, he's bought a headache!

To begin with, the little woman had better be handy with a needle, because any repairs his uniforms need—even if ripped in a tussle with a hoodlum—are paid for out of the cop's own pocket. Same goes for dry cleaning. If he gets bloodstains on his uniform caring for a brother officer shot in a bandit chase, it's his responsibility to have his uniform clean for the next inspection. Technically, the city gives him a uniform allowance for these purposes, of a paltry $125 a year, which, considering today's costs is completely inadequate.

He's always shelling out. Right at the start, his uniforms and equipment set him back about $350. In addition, the cop forks over a minimum of about $400 a year to the Pension Fund and subsequently $527 a year, when he becomes a first-grade patrolman—which is a substantial slice of his income.

He pays the PBA its annual dues, which are little enough, but he is also assessed a monthly "house" tax. This is to provide for linens, etc. used in the precinct house. And, by the time he gets through kicking in, the average take-home pay of a rookie cop is around $73.50.

And for that he risks his life! Even if he gets into a gun battle he has to pay for his own bullets! While the city will ultimately return the cost, a cop would have to be off his rocker to put in a claim for spent bullets.

The only break he gets out of a fight is that if he's hurt, he's provided with the best of medical attention. But, even the ordinary factory worker gets *that*, and without risking his life. And if the policeman takes sick not in line of duty, he is docked one-half pay for the first three days of his illness.

The man who pounds the pavements is, strictly speaking, on 24-hour duty. He has only six paid holidays a year—less than the most menial employee. However, if a holiday comes during his regular tour of duty, he does not get the expected day off, which he can well use. He merely gets paid for the day. The extra pay that he receives is small compensation for forfeiting time with his family.

He's supposed to be on a five-day week, with 48 hours off. The joker is that he's on an hour-to-hour basis. So a white collar worker who quits at 5:00 P.M. on Friday, doesn't show up again until 9:00 A.M. on Monday—*giving him 64 hours free*. On the other hand, the cop gets only 48 hours off.

For example, if he quits at 4:00 P.M. Friday, he's due back on post at 4:00 P.M. Sunday. In addition, the bluecoat can be called in an emergency for overtime services at any time, for which he is only paid straight time for working overtime. Bear in mind, however, that any worker in any industry always gets time and a half for his overtime.

Moreover, the average policeman can never spend too much time at home, because he spends two-thirds of his working life on the force *doing night duty*. Unreasonable? That's the understatement of the year!

When Khrushchev and Castro were in New York visiting the UN, the police department worked overtime an aggregate of one million man hours. They could not have compensatory time off in that case as it would deplete the whole force, so instead, they were paid at straight time, and they worked 7-day weeks for an entire month.

But that's not all that goes on. If, by some mischance, the cop runs afoul of the many regulations (and in these days *everyone* complains), he faces a departmental trial. If found guilty he's fined from half a day's pay up to thirty days or more, depending on the severity of the charges. In other words, he's then required to risk his life for free! The fine, presumably, goes into the pension fund.

That's making the punishment fit the crime—in spades. Even if the cop didn't break any rules, but happened to make an arrest requiring his presence in court, he's still left holding a great big empty satchel. As of this writing, the time he spends in court is his own. And there's always the chance, as so often happens, that some zealous traffic cop will ticket his car while he's in court—because the police department refuses to grant its men special stickers for use on official business!

That's the 'Finest'? Here's another one: On Election Day, all the books and ballot boxes stored throughout the year in precinct houses have to be hauled to polling places by the cops themselves. And, after a 14-hour day, hauled back again. If the cop wants to hire a cab or a truck it's okay with his superiors—as long as he pays for the transportation out of his own pocket. Because the city won't!

So if you want a job that reads like a dream, but is more like a nightmare, it's all yours if you can stand the gaff. Which is why we say pity the New York cop who pounds the pavement for peanuts, and his head in desperation, as he tries to figure out the unjust system that pays the average worker more dough than the cop who risks his life protecting his fellow citizens.